RHINO

Rhino

Daryl & Sharna Balfour

NH
NEW HOLLAND

First published in the UK in 1991 by
New Holland (Publishers) Ltd
37 Connaught Street, London W2 2AZ

ISBN 1 85368 102 4

Editor: Tracey Hawthorne
Designer: Joanne Simpson
Cover designer: Neville Poulter
Illustrators: Philip Huebsch (pages 36, 45, 54, 56, 57);
Dave Snook (pages 62, 71, 76, 77, 78, 79)

Typeset by Diatype Setting (Pty) Ltd
Reproduction by Hirt & Carter (Pty) Ltd
Printed and bound in Hong Kong by Leefung-Asco
Printers Ltd

Every effort has been made to trace the copyright owners of
certain textural and pictorial material in this book, but this has
not always been possible. The publishers would appreciate any
information that would enable them to do so.

HALF TITLE PAGE: *black rhino*
TITLE PAGE: *white rhino*
THIS PAGE: *white rhino*
OVERLEAF: *black rhino*

For our parents, with love and gratitude;
And for the rhinos of Africa –
may they survive to grant future generations
the pleasure they gave us.

Contents

ABOVE AND OVERLEAF: *'Here were two of Africa's most fearsome beasts, almost within touching distance, regarding me with a mixture of curiosity and frightened vulnerability.'*

Acknowledgements

This book would not have been possible without the support and assistance of many people. We extend our thanks in particular to the director and officers of the Natal Parks Board, especially Dr George Hughes, Tony Conway, Apie Strauss, Rodney Henwood, Tom Yule, Trevor Sandwith, Peter Rogers, and Fernando and Tracey Ferreira. Without their active support, this project could not have been undertaken.

We were assisted greatly in our research by the work done by many others, in particular Esmond Bradley Martin and Norman Owen-Smith, to whom we wish to give full credit and many thanks.

Vere van Heerden of Helicon provided invaluable assistance in obtaining the helicopter photographs. Sean and Nina Beneke of SD General Spares, Mhlume, Swaziland gave generous material support in keeping our four-wheel drive on the road, for which we are exceedingly grateful.

Dave Aronovitz of L. Saul & Co Ltd assisted in keeping the battery of Minolta cameras serviceable, and with the loan of certain equipment from time to time, while Peter Icharia of Kodak (Kenya) Ltd ensured the supply of Kodachrome film. Stuart Burmeister of Citylab, Durban provided a truly professional service in processing the E6 film used. We hope the pictures in this book do their efforts justice.

DARYL & SHARNA BALFOUR
HERMANUS 1991

Preface

Anyone who asks me how I became involved with saving the black rhino of Tanzania has obviously not got a 19-year-old daughter!

In 1988 my daughter, Katya, my wife, Jackie, and I were camping in the Serengeti with some scientists who were working on an animal research programme. The evening camp-fire talk turned to the plight of the black rhino. In the previous five years, 90 per cent of the black rhino of Tanzania had been lost to poachers who sell rhino horn to the Middle East for use as dagger handles.

The scientists believed that the black rhino would become extinct if something were not done – and done quickly – to help save it. There was a Tanzanian government scheme to capture the rhino in the vast Selous game park and move them 400 miles north to smaller parks where they could more easily be protected, but it was gathering dust for lack of US $750,000 which was needed to put the plan into action. Sitting by the camp fire, listening to these dedicated people talking, we realized that we were bound to get involved. My daughter, Katya, volunteered my services to raise the funds . . . with the sun setting over the cadmium-coloured plains, the sound of the crickets and the crackle of the logs, I realized that Africa had seduced me.

Once I returned to England, however, I am afraid that life got back to normal, and like my tan my interest faded. So if a single rhino is saved because of any effort made by me, it will be my wife and daughter that it will have reason to thank. Like Tanzanian mosquitoes they nagged and worried me . . . there was no way that I was to be allowed to forget my promise. Six months of worrying and nagging was enough to do the trick, and we founded a charity, the Faith Foundation, whose sole task was to raise the funds for the Tanzanian black rhino project.

In three months we had collected enough equipment and funds to start the first phase of the project. In June 1990, the equipment was shipped to Tanzania. With luck, and a fair wind, our project – an idea which started on a magical evening in the Serengeti – will become a reality, and achieve what some people think already an impossible task: the saving of the black rhino.

Once you get involved with these 'prehistoric' creatures, it is impossible not to become emotionally caught up with their plight. That we are prepared to allow one of the earth's oldest animals to be pushed to the brink of extinction because a handful of us need to emphasize our virility by sporting daggers with rhino-horn handles is a fact that says far too much about the mentality of man. Let us hope that things will change.

The important thing now is to spread word of the plight of the rhino – both those of Africa and elsewhere. Jackie and I are pushing the message here, and Katya has taken the word abroad: at the University of Pennsylvania she hopes to enlist the help of the next generation of American rhino protectors. We all hope that this important book will be widely read. If it helps to gain protection for a single rhino, it will have done its job.

Adam Faith
Chairman
Faith Foundation, London

White rhino

Foreword

IAN PLAYER (DR) DMS

Daryl Balfour is a rare combination of good writer, photographer, observer of the natural world and astute commentator on the political conservation debate about the fate of the rhino. He has written an outstanding book. *Rhino* will quickly become a collector's item. In a conversation with me Daryl modestly referred to his book as primarily a coffee table book. By definition a coffee table book lies around waiting for someone to pick it up and glance at the photographs. *Rhino* is, I predict, a book that is not only going to be looked at, but also widely read and quoted.

Daryl Balfour has succeeded where so many professional conservationists turned writer have failed. He, in a few sentences, slashes away at the rhetoric surrounding the conservation of the rhino and carefully lays bare the bones of the whole problem. It is true that he has been assisted in this task by that indefatigable rhino researcher Esmond Bradley Martin and some other researchers such as Norman Owen-Smith. Daryl Balfour, however, writes a delightfully fresh and direct account of the plight of the rhino.

It is obvious too from the personal experience he has had with white rhino and black rhino that he is a most patient and diligent field worker. As I read through his manuscript I found myself transported back to earlier days when I was a junior game ranger, then senior ranger, rising up the scale to warden and chief conservator for Zululand. In my early game ranging days I spent many weeks in the Umfolozi Game Reserve traversing the country first on foot and later on horseback when there was no further danger from nagana, the disease carried by the tsetse fly. My primary job was establishing game guard camps on the periphery and at selected areas within the reserve. Not a day passed without an opportunity of watching those great, grey, wonderful prehistoric beasts – the white rhino. To lie near a mud wallow on a bright, moonlit night or under the blazing stars of the southern skies while the rhino snuffled like grey ghosts out of the groves of *ntombothi* trees was an experience that endeared these animals to me.

I remember most vividly too my very first view of a white rhino. It was a dull, overcast day and two rhino bulls came out of the mist, grazing on the short grass, their heads moving with a scythe-like motion. I could hear the chomping and when rain spattered on their dark bodies I could smell them, and something deep inside me was touched.

The rhino at that time were at a point where a disaster, natural or manmade, could cause them to become extinct. They had been shot, killed and hounded from Kuruman in the Cape to the Zambezi in the north. They had become rejected beasts and victims of mindless killing in the name of sport and for the products of their dead bodies. I had been through a few hard years since returning from the Second World War, going from job to job until I joined the Natal Parks Board as a relief ranger, a post that no-one wanted. My early feelings of rejection gave me a close sense of personal identity with the rhino. I looked at them as a cause to which I was prepared to give my life, and for the next 12 years I was closely interwoven with their destiny.

For the years 1955-56 then the six years 1958-64 I was in charge of the Umfolozi Game Reserve and became involved in a titanic struggle to extend the borders of the reserve. The 1897 and subsequent proclamations had made the Black and the White Umfolozi rivers the boundaries of the reserve. The Mdindini fist on the south bank of the White Umfolozi River was like a dagger pointing at the heart of the game reserve and I knew that if part of the then southern and western crown lands was not incorporated into the game reserve, as well as the corridor linking the Hluhluwe and Umfolozi game reserves, the white and the black rhino would be in desperate trouble. All the problems were exacerbated by a huge influx of people forced to flee from the Msinga area in the Tugela valley as a result of clan warfare that stemmed from overpopulation and over-utilization of dwindling natural resources.

In my book *The White Rhino Saga* I was unable to describe in any depth the political struggle to incorporate the crown lands. I was an employee of the Natal Parks Board and involved in the political conservation battles and therefore unable to write about the tactics we had used to win the critical areas and have them added to the Umfolozi Game Reserve.

My interest in history had led me to read the memoirs of many generals and one statement was very useful to me: 'Strike when the enemy thinks he has won and then at the point where he least expects it.' We did this many times and, in spite of being only a few, close-knit individuals under the brilliant leadership of Colonel Jack Vincent, we won the day with the southern and western state-owned lands.

Eventually I was able to send Nick Steele, my long-time friend and ranger colleague, a copy of Proclamation No. 53 of 1962. Nick Steele sent a note that I still have. He wrote: 'I can hardly bring myself to believe that after years of the most terrible suspense, this land and its wildlife are safe in the hands of conservation.' Behind this reply lay four years of the most bitter struggle against government departments and individuals who had no feeling whatsoever for wild lands.

This foreword is not the place to tell that story, but I must mention the Corridor because it played a big part in Daryl Balfour's life while he was studying and photographing the white and the black rhino in the wallows, on the hills and in the valleys of this extraordinary piece of beautiful country that linked the two game reserves. By the end of 1963 we had fought that Corridor issue to a standstill. The government had come up with many alternatives for its use, including range land, mining, and an area for coloured resettlement.

We fought back in the press. Although as rangers we were unable to make a statement, we found ways around this problem. We wined, dined and entertained pressmen, radio people and VIPs who could influence events, but it was always the people we could lure away from the camps and their attendant luxuries to the campfire in the bush who became touched by the spirit of the wilderness of Umfolozi and supported our cause.

At the end of 1963 I said to Nick Steele, 'I know in my gut that we have done everything possible to include the Corridor. The issue must now rest in the hands of God.'

In 1966, after an evening of heavy wrangling with a deputy cabinet minister about the squatters who were taking over the eastern section of the Corridor, we persuaded him to let us put up a fence. Douglas Mitchell, the then deputy chairman of the Natal Parks Board, was a tough and skilled negotiator and when the deputy cabinet minister agreed to the fencing, Mitchell turned to me and said, 'Get started tomorrow.' And we did. But it was not until 1989 that the Corridor was legally proclaimed. I was by this time a board member of the Natal Parks Board, the only ex-member of staff so far to have had this honour, and I felt a deep satisfaction when the chairman Dering Stainbank made the announcement. We had won the final battle for the Corridor.

The capture and translocation of the white rhino that began in 1960 and the subsequent re-stocking of parks like the Kruger National Park, Matopos and Hwange in Zimbabwe, Moremi in Botswana and the Maputo Elephant Park in Mozambique, required many hours of hard work. However, the original Operation Rhino team never flagged in its dedication and slowly the numbers of rhino outside the Umfolozi Game Reserve mounted.

In 1970 the Natal Parks Board considered shooting white rhino within the park because despite capture and translocation the numbers continued to grow. I objected, sought an interview with the Board, and after a long fight I was given authority to travel overseas and sell white rhino to the new and expanding open zoos. I went through some desperate moments when zoo directors baulked at buying 20 white rhino at a time, but when the London Zoological Society and the San Diego Zoological Society agreed to buy, it was the beginning of a flood of orders and hundreds of rhino were exported to safe areas. Recently when I went to the San Diego Zoo they told me that there had been 77 births since 1970.

The white rhino story was a model that the rest of Africa should have seized upon and implemented. It failed to do so and Daryl Balfour gives a litany of the stark facts of the demise of black rhino.

I believe most of the blame can be laid at the door of Western and Russian governments. The Western world poured billions of dollars of aid into Africa, but did not insist that a small proportion of the money should be used for conservation. The Russians exported revolution and firearms without a moment's thought of the consequences to wildlife and its habitat. Africa is the keep of big game, but the world watched in virtual silence as the elephant and rhino were slaughtered, then it had the insolence to punish the very countries who did do something. South Africa has received little acknowledgement for its superb efforts to conserve its wildlife for the benefit of mankind. The world looked at South Africa and saw nothing beyond apartheid and minerals. Fortunately in recent years some African countries have realized that South Africa can offer expertise that no-one else can match.

It is tragic that the white rhino twice became extinct in Mozambique. By 1896 it had been shot out by hunters. In the 1960s we in the Natal Parks Board re-stocked the Maputo Elephant Park and the white rhino began to thrive again. In 1974 revolution swept the country and within ten years the white rhino was extinct once more. I have no doubt that South Africa will be called upon to help re-stock when peace finally returns to Mozambique, and will do so. Daryl Balfour's book is a magnificent continuation and expansion of the white rhino story, and he now joins it to the black rhino.

As I read his manuscript I found myself nodding and audibly agreeing with everything he says. He touches on the multimillion-dollar business in rhino products, the bribery and corruption, the controversial cutting of rhino horns in Namibia. He has done a remarkable amount of homework and his incisive comments should be carefully read by wildlife conservation professionals and anyone interested in the fate of the rhino.

Daryl Balfour was born in 1952, the same year that I began walking the rhino paths in the Umfolozi Game Reserve, following much the same route as the early conservationists Vaughan-Kirby and Captain Potter. It was for me the beginning of the most important part of my life. It was also the start of another journey, that of inner exploration, and one that led me to the realization that the wilderness experience was in fact a religious quest. It was this understanding that gave me the inspiration to fight for the setting aside of a wilderness area in the Umfolozi Game Reserve and at Lake St Lucia, another first in Africa by the Natal Parks Board. Since 1959 more than 100 000 people have walked through the wilderness area of Umfolozi led by Natal Parks Board and Wilderness Leadership School trail officers. I believe that an important percentage of these people constitute the central core of the environmental lobby of South Africa today.

Daryl Balfour in a letter to me says: 'My first-ever view of a rhino was as a 10-year-old in Umfolozi back in the mid-60s, when my father brought us and a group of international tennis players to the reserve for a few days. You took us out in your Land Rover and we approached a few whites [rhinos] on foot! It had a profound effect on me as a youngster, and although I have never become the "game ranger" I then vowed to be, the bush and its inhabitants have never been far from my heart. In my photographs and writings, I hope I can render it "as it is".'

Daryl Balfour has fulfilled his rendering 'as it is' very ably in this book. I found his description of one of his first encounters with black rhino intensely moving, and the sense of this pervades all the pages of his book. He writes: 'Here were two of Africa's most fearsome beasts, almost within touching distance, regarding me with a mixture of curiosity and frightened vulnerability. It was, for me, a turning point in my relationship with the rhino we'd come to study and photograph, a moment that I can describe only as deeply spiritual.'

I found this description inspiring. It is the essence of the wilderness experience, without which I believe there can never be any real understanding of what wildlife and wild lands conservation is all about.

For far too long we have had to listen to rational and scientific expositions, very valuable but never the complete story. If there is not an understanding of the heart or spirit of the conservation cause, science alone will be inadequate. It is Dionysian and intuitive feeling we need along with Apollonian, rationalistic thinking.

Daryl Balfour has combined both to produce a remarkable book.

Magqubu Ntombela and Ian Player

Contents

LEFT: *Significantly smaller than the white rhino, the black rhino's outline is also noticeably different; it holds its shorter, more proportionate head erect and is more hollow-backed than the white.*

From The Wild Sports of Southern Africa
by Captain William Cornwallis Harris

Introduction

Two black rhino stood attentively less than 25 metres from where I sat, motionless, on a treeless ridge. The short-sighted animals, a cow and her 30-month-old female calf, probably couldn't see me but they certainly knew I was there.

I'd been following them for several hours but had only approached them closely once they'd settled down for a nap after browsing for most of the morning. Unfortunately there wasn't a sturdy tree in sight − the only cover was a flimsy euclea shrub that certainly wouldn't give much protection against a full-blooded black rhino charge. After observing quietly from behind the shrub for a while, I'd crawled into the open to give myself a clear field of vision and started shooting with the 300 mm lens.

At the first click of the shutter the calf's ears swivelled in my direction. At the second click she lurched to her feet; her mother raised her head with a start, then she too rose to face me. As I continued shooting, they both began to approach. After a quick glance around to confirm what I already knew − that there was no climbable tree in the vicinity − I studied the frail euclea more closely. In a pinch, I supposed; I could scramble into it and gain a height advantage of a metre or so. But an adult black rhino cow stands that at the shoulder . . . and is able to reach a good bit higher with her horn.

I decided to remain silently where I was, reasoning that a move would most likely startle the animals and provoke a charge. I slowly lowered my eyes − I read somewhere once that wild animals can sense your stare and become alarmed by it. A fly crawled busily over my face, but I dared not move to shoo it away. Both rhino raised their heads and sniffed the air, but I was downwind and they could not pick up the human scent that would probably have sent them crashing away. Then they began to make low, grunting, keening sounds to each other, the likes of which I'd not heard before, and after a few moments of this appeared to relax and, it seemed, accept my presence as non-aggressive.

I slowly raised my camera and resumed photographing. Their reactions to the sound of the shutter had become more reassuring: after a few flicks of their radar-like ears their curiosity was satisfied, and the younger of the two turned aside to chew on a fire-blackened sweet thorn (*Acacia karroo*). After gazing myopically in my direction for a few minutes more, the cow too seemed satisfied, and joined junior in browsing while my camera clicked away.

Gradually the two black rhino, by reputation among the most dangerous of all Africa's wild animals, moved closer to where I sat. Both were keeping a wary eye on me, but other than that did not appear too concerned by my presence. When they had approached to within 15 metres I slowly and carefully shifted closer to the flimsy refuge of the euclea shrub, watched all the time by the cow. The 300 mm lens at that short distance was far too long, and I was down to a 35-135 mm zoom lens . . . and grateful for the wide-angle capacity.

Junior, whom I later named Lucy, moved closer to her mother and both animals continued in my direction. I suddenly realized that they seemed intent upon browsing the very bush behind which I was crouching: the rhino were well within 10 metres and approaching steadily. In previous encounters with black rhino I'd found the mechanical sound of my cameras' motordrives had often scared them off, so I slid the switch from 'off' to 'on' and fired off a few quick frames. The rhino barely reacted, however, and I decided that discretion had become the better part of valour. I hoisted myself into the fork of the euclea. Branches creaked and the sapling swayed and shook . . . both rhino looked up from their browsing, but did not even stop chewing.

Realizing these were no ordinary black rhino and that aggression seemed far from their intentions, I cautiously lowered myself to the ground and resumed my photography as the animals moved even closer. By then I was zooming right out to 85 mm, 50 mm, 35 mm, filling the camera frame with the two animals and the expanse of scenery behind them. They were less than three metres from me!

They must finally have come close enough to catch a whiff of human scent, for the calf began to display signs of nervousness. She walked up close beside her mother, then, as if seeking reassurance from each other, the two rhino lowered their heads cheek by jowl, snuffled and sighed, and peered straight at me. It was all I could do to still my shaking and carry on clicking away . . . and a lump formed in my throat. Here were two of Africa's most fearsome beasts, almost within touching distance, regarding me with a mixture of curiosity and frightened vulnerability. It was, for me, a turning point in my relationship with the rhino we'd come to study and photograph, a moment that I can describe only as deeply spiritual.

LUCY

While I was to have countless other close encounters with both black and white rhino during the year we spent in Zululand's famous Umfolozi Game Reserve, none would affect me as deeply as that special meeting. And it was not to be my last encounter with Lucy and her mother. Eventually I came to believe that these two wild animals knew and recognized me in the field, for I was able to work closely with them on several occasions, each time with their apparently totally accepting my proximity.

Six weeks after that initial encounter, Lucy was darted and captured for relocation to another game reserve, and held for a month in a pen, or boma, alongside our camp at the foot of Mpila Hill. During this acclimatization period we came to know each other a bit better, and from day one she would allow me to stretch through the bars of the boma to scratch her ears, and take titbits of fresh browse from my hands.

One morning I took Lucy a cutting of an acacia she did not particularly like. She sniffed it disdainfully through the bars, then proceeded to tell me what she would prefer for breakfast: after scouring the floor of the boma, Lucy brought me a stubby, leafless piece of tamboti (*Spirostachys africana*). I knew she had developed a predilection for the browse of this particular tree, and when she stood on her side of the bars, dry piece of branch jutting from the corner of her prehensile-lipped mouth, and simply stared at me, I got the message immediately. Two minutes later I was back at the boma with a freshly cut branch of tamboti. Lucy took it greedily from my hands, stepped back and chewed it with visible – and audible – relish.

It was a sad day for us when, along with five other black rhino from the Umfolozi Game Reserve, she was taken by road to her new home in the Andries Vosloo Nature Reserve in the eastern Cape. We later heard she was making quite a nuisance of herself because of her partiality to human company; she had taken up residence in close proximity to one of the staff homes, which must have been somewhat disconcerting for the resident.

BEGINNINGS

Rhino are seriously endangered throughout the world today. Only the southern race of the white rhino is out of immediate danger of extinction, thanks to the pioneering efforts of the Natal Parks Board and their now-famous Operation Rhino of the early '60s. The black rhino population, previously the largest of all the rhino species', is being decimated as a result of organized commercial poaching throughout Africa north of the Limpopo River. It seems likely that only the southern African populations will make it into the next century, once again due to the effective conservation efforts of the Natal Parks Board.

It was in early 1989 that we arrived in the Umfolozi Game Reserve and pitched camp in a shady grove of tamboti and schotia trees, having been granted permission by the Natal Parks Board to spend a year photographing rhino in the Umfolozi-Hluhluwe-Corridor complex. Proclaimed a game reserve in 1897 specifically to save the white rhino from extinction, it somehow seemed proper for us to be here.

The previous summer had been a good one of long hot days and plentiful rain, with the result that the red oatgrass (*Themeda triandra*) stood shoulder high. In the initial weeks seeing and photographing rhino was a difficult task, and on several occasions while walking through the valleys of the reserve I all but stepped on the animals as they lay dozing in the autumn sun, screened from view by the towering tangle of themeda.

Gradually, though, I came to know their habits, discover the popular watering points and perennial springs, and determine the territories of the resident white rhino bulls and the home ranges of the black rhino cows and calves, so that I could find my subjects with relative ease.

MONKEY BUSINESS

One morning in May, when the pans had dried up and the grass was beginning to wilt and die, I noticed six white rhino across a valley, grazing on the opposite hillside. I made my way towards them, but could not approach them closely because of the lack of cover and the prevailing wind direction. After a while the rhino moved off, and I was able to follow downwind of them. They gathered on a dusty, dry pan, obviously a popular place with the local rhino as there were numerous rubbing posts (tree stumps worn smooth by rhino rubbing against them) scattered about and a number of rhino paths leading in from all directions. After standing around uncertainly for a few minutes, all six animals lay down and soon appeared fast asleep, although their ears never stopped moving, listening for any alien sound. I began my approach, which necessitated a crawl of some 50 metres across a barren, open area, towards a towering scented thorn (*Acacia nilotica*) which offered good cover some 15 metres from the dozing behemoths. As luck would have it, though, when I was but halfway two of my cameras knocked noisily together and in a flash all six rhino were on their feet and glaring in my direction. I rose to a semi-crouch and darted forward, trying to keep the tree between myself and the considerably agitated rhino. I reached the tree in record time and hauled myself into its lower branches.

'The African Rhinoceros' from Portraits of the Game and Wild Animals of Southern Africa *by Captain William Cornwallis Harris*

This seemed to satisfy the rhino and they relaxed again, as if my tree climbing indicated that I was no threat to them. One by one they settled down and resumed their sleep – all but a large male who ambled over and stood gazing at me, perched uncomfortably among the thorns. He appeared not to be bothered by the sound of my camera and even when I broke off some dead twigs and branches to improve my field of vision he did not start. After watching my antics for about half an hour, he circled back to where the others slept and lay down to rest, though from time to time he'd raise his massive head and look in my direction.

I was to encounter this reaction – or lack of it – from both black and white rhino on numerous occasions and can only assume that by climbing a tree I displayed characteristics unlike those that rhino associate with danger. Perhaps they regarded me as some kind of clumsy baboon!

After watching the sleeping animals for some time, I decided to move on. I climbed down, hoping to sneak away while they slept, but as soon as I reached the ground the bull who'd been keeping his eye on me all along stood up and advanced. I held my ground, but not for long – for with a snort and a toss of his head the bull made a brief rush at me. The other five rhino came to their feet . . . and I climbed back into the tree. The rhino milled around uncertainly less than 10 metres from the base of my refuge, then they took up the defensive position, standing in an outward-facing circle, the large bull almost within touching distance below my perch. I clapped my hands and swore at him, but he merely backed off a few paces and then advanced again. Deciding I'd rather not further agitate the group, I settled back to outwait them . . . and sure enough, after 15 minutes or so they gradually settled down to sleep.

Eventually I plucked up the courage to descend and attempt another escape. This time when the rhino lurched to their feet and rounded on me, I stepped boldly into full view beside the tree, clapped my hands loudly and shouted. Obviously recognizing me as a human for the first time they turned on the spot and rushed off in myopic confusion, tails curled tightly over their rumps and puffs and snorts rending the air – much the reaction I had come to expect from white rhino when suddenly faced with a human being.

WHITE RHINO AND MAN

Despite their size – they are the third-largest land mammals after the African and Indian elephants – and the effectiveness of the heavy horn in defence, white rhino are generally pathetically timid when confronted by man and usually rush off in panic as soon as they see, hear or smell a human. For this reason they have a reputation for docility and passivity quite the opposite of that of the smaller, ill-tempered black rhino. But it is generalizations like these that give rise to accidents, and in fact more injuries have been caused by white rhino than black in recent years.

I certainly had more potentially dangerous encounters with white rhino than with black, though the potential danger probably arose as a result of a lack of respect for the white rhino – the old tale of familiarity breeding contempt. Although the general rule seems to be that a white rhino will rush away from you whereas the black rhino will charge straight at you, problems arise when you encounter a white rhino who doesn't know the rules!

'The White Rhinoceros' from Wild Sports of Southern Africa by Captain William Cornwallis Harris

RHINO RULES

One of my closest shaves occurred late in the year after the early summer rains had fallen and temperatures were beginning to reach their notorious Zululand highs. Along with Natal Parks Board section ranger Tom Yule and an artist from the KwaZulu Bureau for Natural Resources, Julie Carter, I'd spent most of a hot and humid day scouring the hills and valleys of the Nqolothi area for black rhino, with little success. Late in the day we spotted a group of white rhino moving towards a small pan, and as we were all keen to obtain photographs of rhino wallowing, we made our way towards them as quickly as we could. We reached the pan when the animals were still grazing about 30 metres from it, and positioned ourselves to make the most of the afternoon sun and available cover. Tom and Julie chose as cover a sizeable marula (*Sclerocarya birrea*), and I crouched behind a small acacia with a convenient fork in which I could steady my camera lens.

Within minutes of our arrival the rhino, about a dozen of them, were wallowing in the pan and, apart from one young male who appeared to be aware of our presence and kept staring towards Tom and Julie, seemed oblivious to the sounds of our cameras. Taking my eye from the viewfinder for few seconds I noticed a large bull who had not joined the others in the wallow, grazing to the left of the pan and heading in my direction. He was a lovely sight in the lush green grass, his hide catching the late afternoon sun, and I turned my attentions to photographing him. Because I was partly obscured by the trunk of the acacia, the bull did not notice me and continued feeding, moving directly towards me. Using an 80-200 mm lens I was able to keep him in the frame, and it was only when I could no longer focus on him that I realized just how close he'd come. With a start I lowered the camera and the bull, less than two metres from me, suddenly became aware of my presence. There was no way I'd be able to climb into the little acacia, the trunk of which was only about 15 centimetres in diameter, so I decided to sprint to Tom and Julie's tree about four metres away, where they sat oblivious to my plight and still photographing the group in the wallow directly before them. I made my move, hoping that as I appeared in the open the rhino would react as white rhino were meant to, and turn tail in panic.

Unfortunately, the bull hadn't read the rulebook and as I ran he lowered his head and charged. I yelled at him, and Tom, turning and assessing the situation admirably quickly, immediately hoisted Julie into the marula while adding voice to my screams. The rhino veered past as I crashed into Tom behind the marula, fortunately a large tree with several low branches. By then the rest of the rhino had come to their feet and were milling about in uncertainty, and several of the younger animals were eyeing our position with obvious evil intent. The bull wheeled with the agility I always found surprising in such large and clumsy animals and came straight back at us.

I had my camera raised once more, hoping for the ultimate charge shot. Tom, still shouting at the rhino, drew his heavy revolver. Fearing for my eardrums almost as much as for the rhino, I had to forego thoughts of photography and join in the barrage of yells. Once again the rhino skidded past close enough for us to feel the rush of air, but this time the momentum of his charge carried him on into the wake of the rest of the group, which had run into a nearby thicket. The bull turned and gave us a defiant glare when he was about 25 metres away, then trotted slowly into the thicket.

LIVING WITH RHINO

While encounters such as these certainly add spice to the lives of those who spend much time in the wild, close shaves are a rarity, with most wild animals more than content to keep out of the way of their greatest enemy, man. Black rhino are less predictable, though: anybody working with black rhino or in an area populated by them is likely to have more than his or her fair share of narrow escapes.

Over the months we spent living with the rhino we developed a respect and a deep love for these obtuse creatures, and came to the conclusion that the world would certainly be a much poorer place if they were allowed to become extinct. Through this book we hope to be able to share some of these feelings and perhaps contribute in some way to the continued existence of the rhino on our troubled planet.

Rhino past, present and future

'Horns of Rhinoceros Africanus as preserved by Captn. Harris' from Portraits of the Game and Wild Animals of Southern Africa *by Captain William Cornwallis Harris*

Rhinoceros have been on earth for more than 50 million years, though whether they will survive even another 50 years is open to speculation. Fossil records show that there may have been as many as 170 different rhino species through the ages; today, four of the five remaining species are approaching extinction, and even the fifth is not entirely safe.

We have little say in the eventual extinction of the species, for in evolutionary time this is inevitable. Like their close relatives the tapirs of the South American and southeast Asian jungles, rhino are primitive representatives of a line that is approaching the end of its evolutionary cycle. Man can, however, reduce the destructive pressure from his own kind so that the five remaining species of rhino can become extinct in the natural course of evolution many years from now, rather than in the 'geological second' represented by our own brief appearance on earth.

ORIGINS

Rhino belong to the mammalian order Perissodactyla, the odd-toed ungulates, a group that has its origins in the Eocene Period of some 60 million years ago. The only surviving members of this order are the tapirs, five rhino species – the black, the white, the Indian, the Javan and the Sumatran – and the horse family.

All five modern rhino are descended from a common ancestor, though the African line split from the Asian two-horned rhino some 10 million years ago, evolving to feed without cutting teeth and therefore losing the incisors characteristic of its Asian relatives. The black and white African rhino, on the other hand, developed longer, sharper horns for defence. Scientists believe the white rhino separated and evolved from the browsing black rhino about four to five million years ago, with the white species evolving into a true grazing animal able to take advantage of the grassy savannas of the African continent. The Sumatran rhino is the most primitive form of rhino alive today and closely resembles the forest rhino which lived into the last Ice Age, 15 000 years ago.

One of the original, prehistoric rhino, *Indricotherium*, stood six metres at the shoulder, and had a body length of seven metres and a head that measured two metres. It became extinct 10 million years ago. Interestingly, *Indricotherium* had tusks similar to those of an elephant and lacked horns, although it did have the three toes of today's rhino. Another early form of rhino was the largest mammal of all time, *Baluchitherium grangerii*, which lived in what is today Mongolia and became extinct in the Upper Miocene Period as recently as 10 to five million years ago. It tipped the scales at 25 tons.

Fossil remains have indicated that early rhino lived throughout Europe and North America, as well as in their present ranges of Asia and Africa. The 'long-legged' running rhino was predominant in North America some 50 to 40 million years ago. The woolly rhinoceros roamed widely across Europe, including the United Kingdom, from about 15 million years ago, and lived in present-day Siberia until the end of the last Ice Age. This animal often lived in close association with the woolly mammoth and is well represented in European cave art; both were clearly recorded in paintings and engravings by Palaeolithic artists dating back at least 20 000 years. A frozen example of a woolly rhino, complete with hair and skin, was dug out of the permafrost of Siberia in 1799, and several others have been excavated since, including remains dated at 38 000 years old in Worcestershire, England.

Fossils show that the narrow-nosed rhinoceros (*Dicerorhinus hemitoechus*), which probably preceded the woolly rhino, disappeared from the scene about 120 000 to 90 000 years ago. It in turn had replaced the Etruscan rhinoceros (*Dicerorhinus kirchbergensis*). Reconstructions from fossil remains indicate that both these rhino looked not unlike today's animals.

RHINO IN HISTORY

Rhino appear in the history books as far back as the fifth century BC, when the Greek physician Ctesias, serving in the Persian court, described a creature that could be found in India that had 'a purple head and carried a single horn upon its forehead'. By the third century BC live rhino had been captured in the vicinity of Lake Chad in North Africa and put on display in Alexandria. Julius Maternus, a noted Roman explorer of the day, was probably the first European to see a live rhino in the wild after he crossed the Sahara in the first century AD and explored the region around Lake Chad.

In 11 BC it was recorded that Emperor Augustus received a rhino as a gift from an Indian sultan, and that shortly thereafter the Romans began sending out expeditions to West Africa to capture rhino for public display in the Roman arenas. However, after the collapse of the Roman Empire, rhino disappeared from Europe as trade links to the outside world were severed. This led to historians and others throughout the Dark Ages making vague and distorted allusions to the mythical unicorn.

For the people of Europe, there was little distinction between fable and reality and such wonderful superbeasts as unicorns, rhinoceros and others remained little more than figments of the imagination, fed by the tales and recordings of the adventurers of the day.

In 1298 explorer Marco Polo described the Sumatran rhino he encountered on his travels in eastern Asia as unicorns: 'There are wild elephants in the country, and numerous unicorns, which are very nearly as big. They have hair like that of a buffalo, feet like those of an elephant, and a horn in the middle of the forehead which is black and very thick. They delight much to abide in mire and mud.'

The first live rhino recorded in Europe after the collapse of the Roman empire was in 1513 when an Indian ruler delivered a specimen to King Manuel of Portugal. This animal was kept on display in Lisbon for several months, before the king decided to send it to Rome as a gift to Pope Leo X. Unfortunately the ship transporting the rhino was wrecked at sea (some records say the rhino itself smashed the vessel in a paroxysm of fury) with the loss of all lives, but several days later the body of the rhino was washed ashore, recovered, stuffed and forwarded to the Pope anyway.

Most early European myths regarding rhino appear to be of Eastern origin. Some of these are amusingly absurd. It was believed, for example, that rhino were fond of music and perfume, and that a man dressed as a highly perfumed virgin girl was an irresistible lure. If the deception did not work and the rhino charged, the decoy could climb a tree and discourage the enraged beast from further aggression by urinating in its ear. Another common belief of the time was that rhino had no joints in their legs, and thus could not lie down nor rise again after having fallen; in order to sleep, it was said, the rhino would lean against a tree. To capture a rhino, therefore, all that was needed was to induce the beast to lean against a tree that had been sawn half through: the tree would collapse, taking the rhino with it, and the stricken animal would be unable to rise again.

THE DUBIOUS POWERS OF RHINO HORN

Rhino horn has been in demand for centuries and records trace the trade to China and India to the beginnings of the Christian era. It was tradition among the wealthy in China during the T'ang Dynasty (618-907 AD) to present to the Emperor on his birthday intricately carved vessels made of rhino horn, and those that remain as *objets d'art* in collections today show the highest standards of craftsmanship. Because of the dimensions of these carvings it is believed they could only have been made from the horns of African rhino.

With the claimed curative powers of the fabled unicorn horn well established in myth and legend it did not take the Arab traders of the Middle Ages long to realize the profit to be made in supplying rhino horn passed off as unicorn horn from Asia and parts of Africa to the importers of Europe. The horns were either carved into cups, spoons and even salt and pepper sets, or ground into a powder by pharmacists and used to treat a variety of ills and ailments. 'Unicorn' horn was an officially recognized drug in England until 1741, and for centuries before this was much valued as a drug throughout Europe. Queen Elizabeth I kept a horn in her bedroom at Windsor Castle, and it was

'The Horns of White Rhinoceros as preserved by Captn. Harris' from Portraits of the Game and Wild Animals of Southern Africa *by Captain William Cornwallis Harris*

25

one of her most treasured possessions. (Even today, Burroughs-Wellcome, one of the world's biggest pharmaceutical manufacturers, has the unicorn as its trademark.)

The powers ascribed to rhino horn were often no less absurd than those ascribed to rhino themselves, and these myths appear to have been given further credibility by the writings of many of the explorers of the 18th and 19th centuries who encountered rhinoceros on their travels. In his book *Lake Ngami*, Charles John Andersson recorded in 1856: ' "The horn of the rhinoceros," Kolben tells us, "will not endure the touch of poison." I have often been a witness to this. Many people of fashion at the Cape have cups turn'd out of the rhinoceros-horn. Some have them set in silver, and some in gold. If wine is pour'd into one of these cups, it immediately rises and bubbles up as if it were boiling; and if there be poison in it, the cup immediately splits. If poison be put by itself into one of those cups, the cup, in an instant, flies to pieces. Tho' this matter is known to thousands of persons, yet some writers have affirm'd that the rhinoceros-horn has no such virtue.'

Andersson also records that 'the horns of rhinoceros were kept by some people, both in town and country, not only as rarities, but also as useful in diseases, and for the purpose of detecting poison. As to the former of these intentions, the fine shavings of the horns taken internally were supposed to cure convulsions and spasms in children.'

Such beliefs were widespread at the time, and although modern science has debunked the purported medicinal virtues of rhino horn, records of its use appear commonly in many different cultures way back in history. That these beliefs and the resultant demand for rhino horn have had a detrimental effect on world rhinoceros populations is beyond doubt, particularly so with regard to the three Asian species, whose horns are held in higher esteem, particularly among the traditional pharmacists of the Orient.

RHINO TODAY

The causes of the extinction of the early rhino forms − habitat changes and hunting by man − remain the biggest threat to the five remaining species, four of which are in serious danger of being exterminated. Today, only the white rhino exists in comfortable numbers, in southern Africa, though earlier this century its numbers in the region had been reduced to about 50; it was saved from extinction only by the foresight of the government of Natal, which declared the area between the Black and White Umfolozi rivers a game reserve in 1897.

There are fewer than 11 000 rhino of all species left on earth today, and the safety of these is far from assured. Black rhino numbers alone have declined by 95 per cent over the past 20 years, from about 65 000 in 1970 to fewer than 3 500 in 1990. The population of the Javan rhino, the rarest of all, was estimated in 1987 by the Species Monitoring Unit of the International Union for the Conservation of Nature (IUCN) at around 50 animals, surviving in the Ujung Kulon National Park in Java. Figures for the Sumatran rhino have been put by the IUCN at 'between 450 and 900' while the Indian rhino appears more secure with a healthy, and increasing, population of about 1 500 in India and a further well-protected 500 in Nepal. The southern race of the white rhino numbers more than 4 600, but the northern race, now believed to survive only in a remote national park in northern Zaïre and in southern Sudan, totals only 30.

JAVAN AND SUMATRAN RHINO

Neither the Javan nor the Sumatran rhino is well represented in zoos outside of its homeland, and the chance of seeing one in the wild is virtually nil. (A Swiss scientist who spent three years in Gunung Leuser National Park in Indonesia, a stronghold of the Sumatran rhino, saw only one specimen, and that for less than 15 seconds as it walked, totally unexpectedly, past his camp.)

Both Javan and Sumatran rhino were widely distributed throughout Malaysia, Cambodia, Laos, Thailand, Vietnam, Burma and India, as well as Borneo, Java and Sumatra, until the turn of the century: at one time during the 18th century Javan rhino were so numerous that they caused considerable crop damage and a reward was paid by the government to whoever killed them. However, demand for their horns and skin, along with technical improvements to firearms during the 19th century which made hunting easier than ever before, led to their wholesale slaughter. Apart from being hunted for medicinal purposes over thousands of years, the Sumatran rhino has also suffered from habitat destruction by logging of tropical forests and the establishment of rubber plantations in much of its range.

BLACK AND WHITE RHINO

When the early white settlers landed at the Cape of Good Hope in the mid-17th century they recorded the occurrence of black rhino on the slopes of Table Mountain; before European explorers with their guns penetrated the more remote parts of Africa as recently as last century, there probably remained throughout the continent between 750 000 and a million black rhino. They were distributed from Somalia in the east to Mali in the west, and from Ethiopia in the north through Kenya, Tanzania, Malawi, Angola, Zambia, Botswana, Mozambique, Namibia and South Africa, while the white rhino was found in Chad, northern Zaïre, southern Sudan, Uganda and the whole of southern Africa.

Nineteenth-century traveller Richard Burton, in his book *The Lake Regions of Central Africa; A Picture of Exploration*, published in 1860, recorded that 'black rhinoceros are as common as the elephant'. Captain William Cornwallis Harris, an Indian Army officer and noted writer, artist and naturalist who hunted the interior of southern Africa in 1836, wrote in 1840 in *Portraits of the Game and Wild Animals of Southern Africa* that 'When the Dutch first established themselves at the Cape of bon esperance – now nearly two centuries ago, the zwart rhinoster existed in considerable numbers on the present site of Cape Town, along the base of Table Mountain; but within the Colony the species has long since ceased to exist, the remnant having long since fled before the destructive cannonade to which it was subjected.'

Harris goes on to say, however, that black rhino were still 'abundant in the wilds of the interior and I have, during a single day, counted upwards of sixty.' He also encountered white rhino in 'incredible numbers' around this time, though Frederick Courtenay Selous noted less than 50 years later that this animal 'must be almost extinct', and that 'thousands upon thousands of these huge creatures were killed by white hunters and natives armed with the white man's weapons'.

THE SLAUGHTER BEGINS

Hunter and explorer William Cotton Oswell led five hunting expeditions to the interior of South Africa between the years 1844 and 1853 and met with and shot numerous rhino, both black and white. In one season alone he and his companion shot no fewer than 89 of these animals, while Charles Andersson also recorded having shot 'many scores' of rhinoceros. Selous, who also accounted for the deaths of a fair share of rhino (he maintained that the flesh of the white rhino's nuchal hump was superior to that of any other game animal in Africa), later recounted that both black and white rhino were

'The Black Rhinoceros' from Wild Sports of Southern Africa *by Captain William Cornwallis Harris*

'practically exterminated in all the countries between the Limpopo and Zambezi rivers' between the years 1872 and 1890, and that by 1880 rhino had become so scarce in that portion of the continent that the 'traders in Matabeleland then for the first time began to employ native hunters to shoot rhinoceroses for the sake of their horns – no matter of what length'. A trader of the time told Selous that he had supplied 400 Matabele with guns and ammunition for the purpose of shooting rhino, and that his stores always contained 'great piles' of rhino horns, 'often the spoils of over a hundred of these animals at one time'.

In the last century there was little if any protection for the wild animals of Africa, for it was believed stocks were inexhaustible. The slaughter of rhino by early explorers, hunters, traders and their agents was by no means contained only in southern Africa, and virtually any journal describing the travels and experiences of these pioneers in Africa south of the Sahara recounts tales of their exploits in shooting both black and white rhinoceros. Often it seems the presence of rhino was regarded as little more than easy meat for the scores of porters and camp followers, and accounts of several rhino being shot simultaneously abound. Charles Andersson, in *Lake Ngami*, boasts of his deeds 'devoted to the destruction of the denizens of the forest'; he frequently shot as many as eight rhino in one night, slaughtering them as they came to drink at isolated waterholes in parts of northern Botswana. Noted big game hunter Arthur H. Neumann in his book *Elephant Hunting in East Equatorial Africa* recounted in 1898 shooting a black rhino cow with a half-grown calf as a diversion during a delay while waiting to go after elephant, because 'we could see she had a very fine horn'. He later measured it at a metre. (Neumann fails to mention the plight of the unfortunate calf, left to fend for itself in the wilds.)

Just as the slaughter was not restricted to southern Africa, so it was also not restricted to the hands of the white explorers, for in Ethiopia and the Sudan the value of rhino horn had been known long before the arrival of the white man, and horns had been exported via the dhow ports of the Red Sea to the Middle and Far East for centuries. It was the appearance of modern firearms that increased the rate of extermination, for until the 1800s most hunting was done by primitive means, either using traps or running the animals to exhaustion on horseback. By the end of the 19th century East African trading ports were exporting thousands of rhino horns each year, and by 1970 rhino were considered to be extinct in both Ethiopia and central Sudan.

In his book *Big Game Hunting and Adventure: 1897-1936*, Marcus Daly reports that during the years 1927-31 French hunters around Lake Chad armed groups of up to 50 local hunters at a time and sent them out to kill as many white rhino as they could. These hunting parties would return with anything between a half a ton and three tons of horns. A ton of rhino horn represents about 300 animals; taking into account that numerous gangs operated in the region, Daly estimated that well over 10 000 rhino were killed in that period alone.

It was a time of frightening short-sightedness. As famous pioneer conservationist Colonel James Stevenson Hamilton recalls: 'Wild animals existed to be killed with as much profit as possible to the killer, and biltong, then as now, commanded a good price and ready sale. There were no hunting ethics whatsoever. If a man did not succeed in killing an animal he had fired at, the next best thing, for his own glorification, was to have wounded it. "We did not actually get anything today, but I wounded a lot of them," was a quite ordinary remark to hear in a bar, even in 1902.' (*The Conservationists and the Killers*, John Pringle, 1982)

(Today's commercial fishing fleets, as well as some sporting anglers, would do well to take note.)

STEPS IN THE RIGHT DIRECTION

Fortunately, this myopia did not afflict everyone. As early as 1884 President Paul Kruger of the South African Republic was propounding his concept of a wildlife sanctuary in southern Africa – though his audience was not at all receptive. It was not until 13 June 1894 that he was able to proclaim the Pongola Game Reserve, Africa's first game reserve. While this was a bold step for conservation at the time, by that stage both black and white rhino populations in the area had been all but exterminated. (A year earlier the rhinoceros was among animals listed as wholly protected game – a step that was really nothing more than admitting that these animals no longer existed.)

An incident in Natal the following year, 1895, led to the beginnings of rhino conservation. A hunting party near the confluence of the Black and White Umfolozi rivers in Zululand shot and killed six white rhino, an act that so infuriated one concerned citizen, Mr C D Guise, that he wrote a letter that eventually reached the Governor of Zululand, Sir Walter Hely Hutchinson, recommending that a) white rhino be added to the list of protected Royal Game, b) no further licences be issued for the hunting of white rhino, and c) that the range of country in Zululand embracing the habitat of the remaining white rhino be declared a game reserve. The governor set about implementing the recommendations immediately, and in 1897 the Umfolozi, Hluhluwe, St Lucia and Umdhletshe were proclaimed game reserves. (The last-named was deproclaimed in 1907, at which time 23 000 hectares were added to the Umfolozi Game Reserve.)

SAVING THE WHITE RHINO

At the time the Hluhluwe area had a sizeable population of black rhino, not considered to be a conservation priority as they were still widespread and numerous over much of their original range. It was the white rhino, extinct everywhere else in southern Africa and down to a mere handful in the tsetse fly-ridden area between the two Umfolozi rivers, that became the focal point of the conservation effort. In 1911 Frederick Vaughan-Kirby, an experienced African big-game hunter and author of two books about his exploits in East and Central Africa, was appointed Zululand's first game conservator. In 1916 he estimated there were 'between 30 and 40 adult animals [white rhino] actually resident in the reserve, as well as a useful number of calves'. He also recorded a limited number of white rhino residing close to the boundary, but outside of the reserve.

This handful represented the last remnants of the southern white rhino, an animal that 80 years earlier had abounded in the 'incredible numbers' recounted by Cornwallis Harris, that Selous recorded as having reached the stage in the north-western Transvaal where they had increased to the limit of their food supply. (Selous was later to write in *African Nature Notes and Reminiscences*: 'The two white rhinoceros I shot in 1882 are the last of their species that I have ever seen alive, or am ever likely to see, and when I left Africa towards the end of 1892 I fully expected that these animals would become extinct within a short time.')

THE PROBLEMS THAT REMAIN

While the 'golden era' for big-game hunters in southern Africa had come to an end, further north new frontiers were only beginning to open up. East Africa and Uganda, while having introduced fairly strict hunting laws soon after the arrival of the early settlers and adventurers, were not immune to the blunders of the day. With the coming of new settlers and the need for more land, vast tracts had to be opened up . . . and cleared of dangerous wild animals. The famous hunter and game control officer J A Hunter, employed by the colonial game department of Kenya in the 1940s to rid the land of all rhino in the Makueni-Machakos district south-east of Nairobi, was personally responsible for the deaths of 996 black rhino over a period of 19 months, between August 1944 and October 1946. All this so that 50 000 acres could be opened up for agriculture!

Hunter himself queried the slaughter: 'Is it worth killing off these strange and marvellous animals just to clear a few more acres for a people that are ever on the increase? I don't know, but I do know this – the time will come when there is no more land to be cleared. What will be done then?'

With those words, I believe, he touched upon the crux of the problem facing not only the rhino, but all the world's wild animals and wild places: one of the major causes of the decline in the numbers of all species of rhino has been the loss of habitat caused by the clearing of bush and forest for human settlement and agriculture. Unless the growth of the world's population, and particularly that of Africa's, can be curbed there appears to be little hope for wildlife.

From Wild Sports of Southern Africa *by Captain William Cornwallis Harris*

To catch a rhino

The radio crackles into life, the waiting team tenses. 'OK . . . we've got one. East of the track about two kays from your position . . .'

Everyone leaps into action, chase vehicles start up and the mini-convoy moves out. At its head rhino capture warden Apie Strauss guns the battered old Land Rover down the rutted and twisting track, his capture team sitting easily in their bouncing and uncomfortable seats, the grins on their faces wide and excited. Time is of the essence now that the dart has been fired home, the meaning of the message that had come in from the tiny helicopter we can now see hovering overhead. Warden Rodney Henwood and pilot Vere van Heerden are an experienced team, perhaps the most experienced rhino-capture outfit in the world today. It's taken them only about 15 minutes from take-off, soon after sun-up, to find a black rhino and fire the dart into its rump . . . no easy matter when you're in a bucking helicopter and the animal is running hell-for-leather through dense brush under towering thorn trees.

Now it's up to the ground crew, and I reach out to steady myself as Apie swerves the jeep off the track and into the veld, crashing through, over and between scrub, and under the occasional tree which I feel certain is going to end our ride at any moment. Grizzled and tanned

by years under the sun, Apie's eyes are squinting in the early morning light as he attempts to spot the rhino which, the helicopter is now telling him, is only 50 metres ahead. Suddenly we see it, on its side and kicking feebly as it tries to fight off the knockdown drug, M99, that is rapidly infusing into its system.

'Got it!' Apie calls into the radio as we jerk to a stop, the team on the back leaping into action in the job they so obviously love. Apie grabs his medicine box and runs. The rope man is the team member with the best – or worst – job, for it's his function to stalk from behind the often still standing and quite lively animal, slip a heavy rope around a rear leg and tether it to the nearest tree. This time, though, the rhino is already down as he loops his rope around an ankle, and unconscious by the time he blindfolds it.

'We try to keep them down as little as possible, look after them as best we can. That's why it's so important for us to get to the animal as quickly as possible once its been darted, because it could have fallen badly, in a way that could suffocate it or cause permanent damage. And these black rhino are priceless, man, you can't buy one for any amount of money. I'd hate to lose one,' Apie tells me while checking the fallen animal. It's gone down easily but is lying unnaturally, flat on its side. The rest of the team gathers

round and quickly pulls the rhino into a more natural position, forelegs folded neatly under its chest. A rhino in the wild never lies on its side for very long, for its massive weight could cut off the flow of blood both to limbs and to organs.

While Apie goes through his routine, injecting an antibiotic into the dart wound and an ointment into the eyes to prevent them drying out while the rhino is unconscious and thus unable to blink, all the while keeping a check on blood pressure and other vital signs, a heavy recovery truck arrives and quickly offloads a large reinforced wooden crate. This operation is so slick it's hard to describe, for the Natal Parks Board, which pioneered rhino capture in the 1960s during Operation Rhino, has designed and had purpose-built a fleet of recovery vehicles ideal for the task. Usually the heavy crate would be slid off the back of the truck so its door is less than a metre from the rhino's nose, but today we'll have to 'walk' the drugged animal into the box from where it's lying about 30 metres away – a steep slope has prevented the truck from approaching any closer.

Knowing the black rhino's temperament, I'm sceptical and grab a camera, heading for a good vantage point. Apie has removed the rope from the rhino's rear leg and slipped it over its head, just

30

Veterinarian Dr Peter Rogers and rhino capture warden Apie
Strauss of the Natal Parks Board Game Capture Unit prepare the
hypodermic darts prior to the capture unit moving into action.
The use of helicopters and specially constructed recovery vehicles
has made rhino capture dramatically easier than it was in the
early days, when darting was done on foot and follow-ups on
horseback.

behind the posterior horn, securing the
blindfold at the same time. After mixing
the antidote, M50 50, or Diphrenorphine
hydrochloride, he slides a needle into a
vein in the rhino's ear and injects just
enough to partially awaken the animal.
In less than a minute the rhino struggles
to its feet, and the team begins to walk it
gently forward, tugging at the rope as if
the rhino were a reticent dog on a lead.
A few times the rhino stops and appears
to want to take its own direction, but a
firm pull on the rope brings it back into
line and soon its head has entered the
door of the crate. The rope is passed
through a hole in the front of the crate,
and other members of the capture team
stand ready to slam the doors closed as
soon as the rhino is in. Apie injects the
rest of the antidote and, giving the animal
a slap on the rump, shouts to the rope
men. With a quick pull the rhino is
inside the box, the doors securely bolted,
and another job well done.

Loading the crate takes only a few minutes as it is winched up on to the back of
the six-ton, four-wheel-drive truck on
custom-made tracks . . . And the radio
crackles into life again: 'Are you finished
down there? . . . we've got a couple of
them here!'

And off we go again.

Later, when we're gathered around the
fire, Rodney Henwood goes over the day's
activities. We've got three black rhino,
and a young white for good measure, and
the action has been non-stop. Now the
weary team can relax for a while. The
following day we'll all be up before first
light to continue the operation, which
will see six black and a great many more
white rhino caught for relocation over the
following two weeks.

'Rhino capture today is a lot more
sophisticated, and easier, than in the early
days when Ian Player, Jim Feely and
Dr Toni Harthoorn were pioneering it.
The helicopter has been a major development, of course, and the newer drugs.
The special capture unit vehicles have
made loading the animals a pleasure; in
the early days it was all done manually,'
says Henwood.

Today, after much experimenting in the
'60s, the most commonly used drug is
M99, used in a 'cocktail' of Fentanyl
citrate and the tranquillizer Azaperone
tartrate for black rhino, with Hyoscine
hydrobromide substituted for the latter
in white rhino.

'We find this cocktail puts the animals
down as quickly as possible with the
fewest after-effects. They would stay
down for about three hours without
antidoting them, though we can top up
the M99 if we need to keep them out for
longer. We do try to keep them down for
as little as possible though,' explains

Henwood. It is interesting that despite
the difference between the two species in
size and body weight, the capture team
uses exactly the same amount of the
knockdown drug for both; even more
remarkable, a tiny duiker requires four
times as much M99 as a rhino!

The temperamental differences
between black and white rhino are
reflected in their behaviour in response to
being darted and subsequently given the
antidote. The black rhino regains its feet
some 60-90 seconds after the injection of
the antidote, and is immediately wide
awake and full of aggression, liable to
charge anything that moves. The white
rhino, on the other hand, remains dopey
and shows lowered responsiveness for
several hours.

The apparent ease and obvious profes-
sionalism with which this rhino capture
operation was carried out makes it hard to
envisage the hardships and difficulties the
pioneers of rhino capture went through,
but as Ian Player writes in his book *The
White Rhino Saga*, it was 'a long hard task
with many disappointments'. It was the
dedication of that original band of men
and their determination to save the white
rhino that today has given hope for the
future of the black rhino, for their successful capture and relocation or reintroduction into areas of suitable habitat is
most certainly a major key to their survival.

The capture and relocation of rhino has been regarded as a prime means of their conservation since the pioneering days of 'Operation Rhino' in Zululand in the 1960s. Today there is hope that the dramatic drop in black rhino numbers can be halted and eventually reversed through capture operations, both to relocate animals away from danger zones and to reintroduce them to areas where they once existed. Thanks to improved immobilizing drugs and the use of helicopters – regarded by capture officers as perhaps the biggest advance in game capture techniques – a number of rhino may be located and captured in a single day.

The relocation of black rhino in particular is an exacting task, for not only must the darting officer, precariously perched in a tiny, swirling helicopter, fire home the dart from a not-too-accurate gas-powered rifle, he must also accurately determine the age and sex of the target before doing so. Once the animal has gone down, usually within minutes of the dart slamming into its rump, the chase team and recovery crew move into action. It is important that the team get to the fallen animal as soon as possible, for it may be lying awkwardly, in a manner that could cause harm or even result in death.

Working with a slickness that comes only through experience, the team rolls the unconscious rhino into a natural position while veterinarians constantly monitor its respiration rate and blood pressure, treat any wounds, and give the animal a general check-over. Should the animal for any reason not measure up, an antidote is administered and it is set free.

Every attempt is made to keep the drugged animal in as natural a state as possible: it is made to lie as a sleeping rhino would and its body temperature is kept down with regular dousings of water. To aid in research, blood and tissue samples are taken, and in most instances, with black rhino, a specially devised numerical code using notches and holes is cut in the ears, enabling the animal's future progress to be monitored.

Often, where a rhino has fallen in terrain too difficult to reach by vehicle, a partial antidote is administered and the semi-conscious animal, blindfolded and led by a rope, is walked out and into the waiting crate, the remainder of the antidote being injected before the doors are slammed closed. The difference in temperament between the black and the white rhino is well illustrated by their reactions to the tranquillizing drugs: the black rhino awakens and is full of fire and anger within 60-90 seconds of the antidote being administered, while the white rhino, although awake, remains dopy and lethargic for several hours.

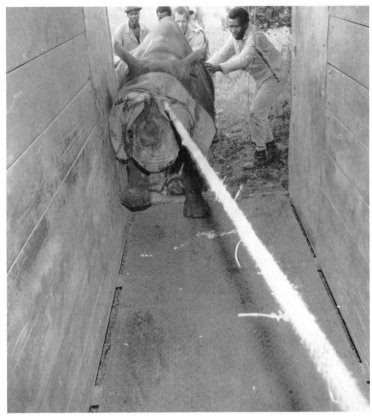

The big five

CLASS: Mammalia
ORDER: Perissodactyla
FAMILY: Rhinocerotidae

SCIENTIFIC NAME	Ceratotherium simum	Diceros bicornis	Rhinoceros unicornis	Dicerorhinus sumatrensis	Rhinoceros sondaicus
COMMON NAME:	White	Black	Indian	Sumatran	Javan
STATUS: (approximate numbers)	4 600	3 500	2 000	400-900	50-60
LENGTH (m):	3,6-4,2	3,0-3,8	2,1-4,2	2,5-2,8	3,5
HEIGHT (m):	1,5-1,85	1,4-1,8	1,1-2,0	1,0-1,5	1,8
WEIGHT (male): (kg)	2 100-3 000	995-1 360	1 500-2 000	800	1 300
LENGTH HORN (cm):	95-200	50-135	20-61	25-80	25-27

The five remaining rhinoceros species, although all descended from a common ancestor, differ widely from one another in appearance, size and behaviour. None can be regarded as common, though the two African species, the white and the black, are at present far more numerous than the rarer Asian varieties – the Indian, Sumatran and Javan. Only the black, white and Indian rhino have been successfully studied in the wild, the other two having proved too elusive for thorough observation.

The white rhino

The white rhinoceros, *Ceratotherium simum*, is by far the most numerous of all extant rhino species, although its northern race with only about 30 individuals in existence is the rarest of them all. The population of the southern race has not always been so healthy, however: had it not been for the actions of a handful of dedicated and far-sighted conservationists less than 100 years ago, the white rhino in all likelihood would have long since become extinct. Today, according to IUCN statistics (1989), the southern race of the white rhino, *C.s. simum*, numbers in excess of 4 600 animals and appears comfortably out of immediate danger. The northern race, *C.s. cottoni*, is 'in immediate danger of extinction', with 26 animals having been recorded in the Garamba National Park in Zaïre in 1990, and four in southern Sudan. By comparison, as recently as 1980 the northern race numbered about 400 in the Sudan, 20 in the Central African Republic, one in Uganda and 400 in Zaïre. In 1989 the Convention on International Trade in Endangered Species of Wild Fauna and Flora (CITES) listed *C.s. cottoni* in Appendix I and *C.s. simum* in Appendix II (see page 75).

SAVING THE SOUTHERN WHITE RHINO

The success story of the southern white rhino culminated in its being removed in 1965 from the Category A protection list of the IUCN ('threatened with extinction') and declared 'no longer endangered', the only animal ever to achieve this distinction. The road to success was not an easy one, however. Early conservationists in Natal had to battle through years of prejudice as well as the government's 'Operation Game Extermination', the wholesale slaughter of any game (except rhino, hippo and nyala) which followed findings by the Division of Veterinary Education and Research in 1916 that there was 'a definite connection' between wild game and the diseases of nagana and sleeping sickness carried by the tsetse fly.

Another setback came when settlers in the area called for the deproclamation of the Umfolozi Game Reserve, and in 1920 this was acceded to. However, the white rhino held in the reserve, estimated at between 30 and 40 adult animals and a handful of calves and representing the last remnant of the subspecies in southern Africa, were the trump card and the Umfolozi Game Reserve was given a stay of execution. Meanwhile, the war against the tsetse fly waged on, and in September 1928 it was announced that bush clearance and the wholesale slaughter of game were to commence. Seven teams of hunters, each with 10 assistants, were set to the task, with instructions to kill all game outside the Umfolozi Game Reserve and to 'thin out' the population inside. In 18 months, 26 539 wild animals were killed by the official extermination squads in and around the reserve. No record was kept of those killed by private hunters.

Fortunately, the white rhino were excluded from the slaughter, although the huge animals were regarded as mobile tsetse breeding stations and were roundly cursed by those engaged in the extermination programme. 'As long as there were rhino, there would be tsetse. And, some officials sighed, as long as there were rhinos there would be sentimental fools fighting for Umfolozi. If only the damn rhino were found somewhere else,' records John Pringle of contemporary attitudes in his book, *The Conservationists and the Killers*.

In September 1931 the Minister of Agriculture, General JCG Kemp, facing yet another anti-nagana conference, maintained that the only way to eliminate the tsetse was to eliminate its hosts, the wild game and the game reserves. 'The white rhino can be protected at Umfolozi, but the rest of the game there must be reduced . . . Settlers and game cannot coexist. One must give way to the other,' he said (*The Conservationists and the Killers*).

With such prevailing attitudes it may be regarded as little short of miraculous that any game at all survived. It was primarily through the efforts of bodies such as the Natal and Zululand Game Protection Association and later the Wildlife Society of Southern Africa, as well as several concerned individuals, that the slaughter was stopped before all wild game in Zululand was completely exterminated. (It was many years later that the discovery of the chemical pesticide DDT and aerial and ground spraying was to go a long way towards the eradication of the tsetse fly and bring the killing to an end.) When control of the Umfolozi and Mkuzi game reserves was finally handed back to the Natal Parks Board after the anti-tsetse campaigns had been completed, the Umfolozi was so devoid of wildlife that, on seeing any antelope or other game, rangers would tip their hats and offer congratulations to the wily survivors!

Through all this the white rhino population was steadily increasing in numbers, from the 30-40 recorded at the turn of the century to some 200 counted in 1929; the first accurate aerial census of 437 was recorded in the Umfolozi Game Reserve by Ian Player in October 1953. By 1960 they had multiplied to such an extent (numbering 705) that capture and relocation to other areas where they had occurred previously was considered necessary. In the first 10 years of this programme, known as Operation Rhino and recounted admirably by Player in his book *The White Rhino Saga*, more than 1 100 rhino were caught and sent to game reserves, parks and zoos throughout the world. Notwithstanding that considerable takeoff, an aerial count in the Umfolozi Game Reserve in August 1970 showed a population of 1 764 white rhino. Today's world population of 4 600, all descendants of the original Umfolozi population and including about 200 in zoos across the globe, represents one of the greatest success stories in conservation – and gives hope for the future of the seriously endangered black rhino.

HOW THE WHITE RHINO GOT ITS NAME

The white rhino was first described to science by the naturalist and explorer William John Burchell, who collected 10 specimens near Kuruman in the northern Cape in October 1812. Burchell's drawings and notes were published by a French zoological society in June 1817. Of course, the native peoples had known of them for many hundreds of years before that, depicting them in their rock paintings from the Drakensberg of Natal across the subcontinent to the Tsodilo Hills of northern Botswana and the Naukluft of Namibia.

The largest of all living rhino species, and indeed the third-largest land mammal after the African and Indian elephant, the white rhino is no more white than the black rhino is black, although the colour was described by Cornwallis Harris as a 'dirty brownish white' as opposed to the 'olive brown' of the black rhino. Certainly the two rhino cannot generally be distinguished by colour alone and in most cases assume the colour of the soil of their surroundings, in which they wallow regularly. However, from the fact that the early Dutch settlers referred to the two species as 'witte renoster' and 'zwart renoster', I can only conclude that it was indeed upon a colour basis that differentiation was originally made, rather than the view that 'white' comes from an anglicization of 'weit' or 'wyd', describing the wide mouth.

William Cornwallis Harris offers a colourful if not entirely accurate description of the white rhino in *Portraits of the Game and Wild Animals of Southern Africa*: 'Attaining a height of nearly seven feet at the shoulder, and carrying a cranium not very dissimilar to a nine gallon cask; he flourishes upon the extremity of his square and truncated snout, a formiddable weapon some three and a half feet long, fashioned after the approved method of a cobbler's awl, and capable, when wielded by a warrior so unquestionable in pith and renown, of being made to force its way through any opposition . . . Superadding to the almost impenetrable folds of shagreen wherein nature hath encased his ribs, a goodly outer coat acquired by constant wallowings in swamps and stagnant pools, the gentleman is but rarely to be viewed under his true complexion, which if not quite so blond as the prefix to his cognomen might indicate, is yet much fairer than that of his swarthy congener, and often approaches to cream colour.'

Norman Owen-Smith, in his definitive thesis on white rhino, *The Behavioural Ecology of the White Rhino*, states that the white rhino of Zululand is a 'dull battleship grey while the black rhino is a darker brown-grey'.

Although many attempts have been made to have the more accurately descriptive terms 'square-lipped' for the white and 'prehensile-lipped' or 'hook-lipped' for the black rhino brought into common usage, this has been to little avail.

DIMENSIONS AND CHARACTERISTICS

The white rhinoceros is essentially a grazing animal, its broad, square-lipped mouth with its hardened, pad-like lower lip having evolved specifically for the purpose of cropping short grasses, as has its typical head-down stance. From a distance it is this stance that immediately distinguishes it from its smaller cousin the black rhino, along with its longer, narrower head and the pronounced nuchal hump on the back of its neck.

Natal Parks Board capture officers estimate the weight of an adult white rhino male at between 2 000 and 2 260 kg, while a young adult sectioned and weighed in the field during Operation Rhino tipped the scales at 2 130 kg. I think these estimates may be slightly low: the heaviest recorded weight for a hippopotamus is 2 660 kg, and I have yet to see a hippo as big as some of the territorial bulls I observed in the Umfolozi. I would deem accurate figures which put the weight of white rhino at 2 100-3 000 kg.

In anybody's terms they are huge animals, prehistoric in appearance and fascinating in their behaviour. Almost passive in their placidity, their first reaction to danger is to run rather than stand and fight, a characteristic that more than frustrated my efforts to photograph them: once they'd discerned my presence, nine times out of 10 they would run away, tails curled comically over their rumps. They are not to be underestimated, however; as Ian Player once said, 'they are harmless animals, but they can get confused and run over you.'

The white rhino has poor eyesight but this differs quite considerably from one individual to another: on many occasions I was able to stalk quite openly to within 30 metres of my subject, being careful to remain below the skyline and to move directly towards the rhino, while on others I would be detected immediately at 100 metres and beyond. Movement seems to be the giveaway, however; they appear able to detect movement at ranges from 30 to 100 metres, depending on the individual animal and the light. I often had white rhino walk up to where I sat motionless on the ground and become aware of my presence only from the sound of my camera, and on two occasions I had to beat a hasty retreat when small calves approached, apparently intent on physically investigating me. The proximity of their mothers on both occasions made me avoid the encounters. Both times the calves were within touching distance and I was totally exposed, seated behind a photographic tripod on the ground.

Their acute hearing and sense of smell serve them well where their eyesight fails them: the volume of their nasal passages is greater than that of their brain. They react immediately to human scent, even where one has merely walked across a path some time before. One afternoon as I traversed a ridge in the Corridor, on the trail of a pair of black rhino, I saw in the distance, across a valley, five white rhino fast asleep under a shady umbrella thorn (*Acacia tortilis*). They were downwind of me and I watched to see if they would react, despite their being at least a kilometre distant. Sure enough, when I was opposite them, directly upwind, they awoke and fled in panic. Owen-Smith states in his thesis that white rhino rely largely on their sense of smell for orientation and knowledge of their surroundings, and records following a white rhino bull that was able to track down a female he'd left one-and-a-half hours previously, following her scent along a trail for 700 metres.

On one occasion, early in our stay, I was to get an indication of just how good is the rhino's hearing. We had set off from camp in the four-wheel-drive before first light, and had stopped in the Gcoyini catchment area to scan the hills for our quarry. Sharna noticed a white rhino cow accompanied by a very small calf grazing under the trees in the valley and, grabbing my cameras, I set off to catch them in the glorious early morning light. At first all went well as I made good use of the cover provided by the waist-high themeda grass. The wind was in my favour and both animals appeared engrossed in their breakfast. I was about 50 metres away when the cow suddenly raised her head and stared in my direction, alerted, I'm sure, by the sound of the grass brushing against my clothing. I froze on the spot, and had to endure a wait of about 20 minutes before she settled back to her grazing. As I prepared to move forward again I inadvertently bumped two cameras together, producing a barely audible clink. The rhino needed no further warning: they turned and literally high-tailed it out of there. I soon learnt that maintaining utter silence was the most important aspect of approaching rhino (other than, of course, remaining downwind), even at distances far greater than usual with other wild game, and would frequently have to remove my boots in order to make a silent approach over difficult ground.

Rhino are not always so alert to sounds though, in particular when feeding in a group. Obviously the sounds they make tearing the grass and chewing noisily, feet scuffing in the dirt, mask other noises. It is once you have their attention that not the slightest sound can be made without eliciting some kind of response.

WHITE RHINO AND THEIR ALLIES

All rhino appear to derive great delight from wallowing. While this certainly serves practical purposes, I like to think that it is also partly hedonistic! During the many hours I spent watching and photographing both black and white rhino in their wallows the overriding impression I received was one of childlike pleasure and satisfaction. As the rhino approached the wallow a jauntiness would animate their usual shambling gait and in many cases they would break into a trot, squealing and uttering all manner of sounds I could only presume communicated anticipation and glee. They then appeared to test the consistency of the mud, often pushing their lower lip or a forefoot into the mire, before entering and plopping down. A sigh would then be heard, and the satisfied animal would lie on one side for a few minutes, apparently relaxing in pleasure, before continuing its ablutions, often rolling right over on to its back, feet kicking skywards. This would be followed by long periods of inactivity, and on hot days the rhino would sleep for hours on end immersed in the wallow, waking from time to time to roll over and muddy their other side. The wallows appear to be social meeting points, and I frequently observed black and white rhino sharing pools with each other, as well as with other animals such as buffalo and warthogs.

The primary function of wallowing is probably to reduce the irritation caused by ticks and biting flies, although the secondary function of heat regulation appears almost as important. Certainly in hot weather you are far more likely to find rhino in wallows than during cold weather, though I did observe rhino wallowing in the rain and on cool overcast days. On a few occasions I noticed terrapins alongside the flanks of rhino lying asleep in a wallow, feeding on ticks and also at the bloody lesions common to black rhino.

Immediately after wallowing the rhino would spend time rubbing themselves against suitable trees, stumps and rocks, again apparently obtaining great satisfaction from the activity but probably primarily to remove ticks and other ectoparasites. Studying such a rubbing post immediately after a rhino had used it would frequently reveal a number of dead or dying ticks. Both African rhino are generally infested with both ticks and flies, some of which are in fact specific to the species. As a result the animals are frequently accompanied by both redbilled and yellowbilled oxpeckers (*Buphagus erythrorhynchus* and *B. africanus*), commonly referred to as tickbirds or rhinobirds (the Afrikaans name is *renostervoël*) and insectivores such as the forktailed drongo (*Dicrurus adsimilis*). I also saw pied crows (*Corvus albus*) on several occasions, strutting over the back or side of sleeping rhino and picking at lesions and ticks, the latter primarily where they congregated under the animals' tails.

The relationship between these birds and the rhino is mutually beneficial, particularly in the case of the oxpeckers, for apart from the obvious interchange of the birds getting a meal while the rhino has annoying parasites removed, the birds act as an efficient early warning system which, as anybody who has worked with rhino will aver, is irritatingly effective. In fact I believe that when accompanied by oxpeckers the rhino afford themselves some respite from being constantly alert, safe in the knowledge that should danger in the form of man appear the birds will give the alarm. I cannot recall on how many occasions oxpeckers forced me to give up a stalk, or sit and wait for them to leave. (Oxpeckers apparently do not give the alarm at any intruders other than man.) On the other hand, the sudden shrill alarm calls of a flock of oxpeckers can give man early warning of the presence of rhino, particularly when in thick bush — very useful in the case of black rhino especially.

WHITE RHINO SOCIETY

Unlike most other ungulates rhino are not gregarious, although the white rhino is commonly found in small groups, sometimes numbering three to 10 and on occasion even more. I found that these aggregations were usually temporary groupings and that the only bondings of any permanence were those between mothers and their calves, and that usually lasting only until the birth of the next calf. The older calf does on occasion rejoin its mother after the birth of the new calf. Older cows, in many instances perhaps those no longer of reproductive ability, were also regularly seen in company with each other, and often in the capacity of 'aunties' with subadult animals. On several occasions I found cows with severe cases of what I later learned was a form of mastitis, which rendered them incapable of suckling a calf; in all cases these animals appeared to have formed a lasting bond with another rhino and I saw them together on numerous occasions through the year. Often several subadults of both sexes will group together after leaving their mothers, and may stay together until adulthood.

White rhino bulls are fiercely territorial, although every bull does not have its own territory and adult males can thus be separated into dominant (or alpha) and subordinate males. A territory averages one to two square kilometres (Owen-Smith), and the territorial bull will not leave his range other than to move directly to and from water if it is not available within the territory; research has shown that the territorial bull will never leave his home range for grazing purposes, no matter what the season, and these bulls can sometimes be seen in appalling condition at the end of a long dry spell when the availability of feed in his territory is poor. Territorial boundaries, which often take the form of natural features but never roads (Owen-Smith), remain unaltered even when a territory changes holder with the death or defeat of the dominant bull. Often territorial boundaries adjoin at major watering points, and these boundaries are patrolled on a regular basis, the holder spray-urinating repeatedly to mark his area. Cows do not display territoriality and there appears to be no connection between individual cows and territorial bulls, with cows frequenting the territories of as many as seven males in their wanderings.

Bulls defend their territory with a variety of intimidatory poses and bluffs, squeals, snorts and snarls. These visual and vocal displays appear to be highly ritualized and fights are rare, rhino having an apparent strong aversion to physical violence, probably because of the high risk of serious injury to both opponents. Disputes thus involve a peculiar display of advancing and retreating in turn by opposing bulls, to demonstrate relative spatial dominance and perhaps avoid loss of face by either opponent. While neighbouring bulls do not actively seek encounters with each other and often seem almost embarrassed if they meet accidentally while patrolling their borders, territorial transgressions are not tolerated.

To the observer, conflicts between white rhino bulls appear highly confusing, with the territorial bull usually being the first to move away, apparently in submission. According to Owen-Smith, who spent seven years studying white rhino in the Umfólozi Game Reserve, the apparently vicious snarl display indicates that the performer is not challenging, even though it is sometimes accompanied by advancing steps and horn-prodding gestures, and appears strongly threatening and intimidatory. Cows, adolescents and subordinate males always meet charges by territorial bulls with snarls and apparent aggression, while the territorial bull (and presumably challengers for territoriality) remain silent. Thus by this snarling display (or lack of it), a territorial bull is able to confirm the status of the challenged animal and modify his actions accordingly. According to Owen-Smith's findings, the fact that the dominant bull is the one who moves away is the only possible termination of the meeting because the subordinate bull refuses to move away as it has no safe refuge in a territory of its own. 'An attack by the territorial bull would only draw forth defensive reponses from the subordinate bull and expose the territorial bull to the risk of receiving injuries himself, as well as drain his energy,' Owen-Smith reasons. 'Having asserted his authority he's won a psychological victory and need waste no further time nor energy.'

One afternoon I was seated at a wallow below Msasaneni Ridge watching a group of four white rhino enjoying a mudbath. Suddenly I heard snorting, snarling and shrieking in the brush beyond the wallow, followed shortly by the appearance of a second group of four white rhino and a large white rhino bull. The second group went off to its own corner of the wallow and the bull, after watching them go, moved down to where the original four were standing. As the bull approached, two much younger males left the group and appeared to challenge the new male, whom I had identified as the resident territorial bull, having seen him on previous occasions. The young males were both snorting and shrieking, producing a sound almost like the trumpeting of elephants, and they curled their lips as they jabbed their horns, heads held high, at the intruder. Certain I was about to witness a clash of Titans, I readied myself and my cameras. The dominant bull moved closer to the young males and for several moments they appeared to have reached a stalemate as the three animals stood almost horn to horn and stared at each other, tails tightly curled over their rumps. Then, as suddenly as it had all begun, the big bull turned haughtily away and ambled over to a section of the wallow slightly further off, where he slumped down with obvious satisfaction. The two subordinate males looked quite disconcerted for some while, then they too returned to their ablutions and peace was restored.

On another occasion when I was out walking with wildlife artist Philip Huebsch, we encountered two large white rhino males competing for the attentions of a female. The horn-to-horn stares were taking place, accompanied by frequent brief clashes of horns, fencing and jousting. Back and forth the two bulls rumbled, producing a range of snorts and snarls, pants and wheezes. One bull appeared to have the inside track, however, and seemed to be intent on keeping the other away from the cow. From time to time all three would settle into a state of torpor, standing head-down and motionless, then the second bull would attempt to manoeuvre himself closer to the cow and precipitate a short rush by the other bull. After well over an hour of this to-ing and fro-ing by the males, the cow (who had appeared totally bored throughout) lay down. Expecting the males to take the opportunity to finally settle their differences, we were amazed when first one bull then the other casually lay down to sleep too, as if a truce had been called for the important business of resting to be undertaken. Interestingly, throughout the encounter there were no signs of serious violence on either bull's part.

When fights between bulls do occur they are generally settled without much ado, although on occasion serious injuries are suffered and in some cases death is the result, for the rhino's horn is an effective and lethal weapon. During our stay in the Umfolozi Game Reserve there were several deaths of white rhino which were attributed to fighting, including at least three where the combatants had been pushed or had stumbled over a precipice and thus fallen to their deaths. A group of visitors on a wilderness trail noticed two rhino fighting atop a cliff alongside the White Umfolozi River, and stopped to watch. The fight had been proceeding back and forth for some time when one bull apparently turned tail to flee. He crashed headlong down the steep slope above the cliff and, appearing unable to stop his passage, plummeted over the edge of the precipice to his death some distance below. As if this were not enough for the startled trailists, the second rhino proceeded to give an instant replay, following the first down the slope and over the cliff to his own death!

Territorial bulls do, however, show tolerance towards subordinate bulls within their territory. As long as the subordinates do not attempt to interfere with a female in oestrus, nor challenge the territorial imperative of the holder, they are accepted. Bulls who have lost their territory to another, younger or stronger animal are allowed to remain in the territory, but with the downgraded status of a subordinate.

DUNG-SCATTERING

White rhino make use of communal middens, or latrines, which territorial animals also use to demarcate their territory. The dominant bull, upon defecating at such a midden, will scatter the dung by kicking backwards with his hind feet, in so doing leaving his own scent spread over the entire heap.

The African legend which explains this dung-scattering action has it that many, many years ago a rhino and an elephant challenged each other to a contest to see who could deposit the largest heap of dung. Although the elephant has by far the bigger appetite, in this tale the rhino won, and in so doing enraged the elephant. The elephant, a poor loser, proceeded to beat the rhino with his trunk and gore him with his tusks until the rhino begged for mercy, avowing that the elephant was the greatest of all creatures. Mollified, the elephant made the rhino promise never again to challenge his might or superiority. The rhino never forgot that terrible beating, and so scatters his dung in order that it may never look bigger than that of the elephant.

White rhino dung is easily discernible from that of the black rhino: the grass-eating white rhino's dung is clearly comprised of grass fibre while that of the black rhino is coarser and made up of pieces of twigs, leaves and bark.

VOCALIZATIONS

White rhino are quite vociferous creatures; many was the time we were woken by the sounds of rhino squealing in the night. Ten discernible sounds, six vocal and four aspiratory, are recognized and all have different meanings (Owen-Smith). Snorts and snarls are interpreted as 'stay away' warnings, the former milder than the latter, while the hoarse, open-mouthed panting functions as a contact-seeking call that draws attention to the performer. A gruff squeal, throaty and rumbling and rising in pitch, is usually uttered by a territorial bull engaged in pursuing another rhino intruding on his range. A high-pitched squeal, almost a singing wail, is usually made by a territorial bull attempting to dissuade a cow in oestrus from leaving his territory and is made in the context of 'boundary blocking'. A shrill, vocal shriek is usually made only by a territorial bull out of his own territory, and subordinate bulls, and signifies conflict between bulls; the shrieks appear to inhibit physical attack.

When suddenly alarmed or frightened, the white rhino makes a 'gasp-puff' sound, like a sudden inhalation of breath, while calves in distress give a short, high-pitched squeak, usually when separated from their mothers or attacked by dominant bulls. A calf seeking to suckle from its mother, or when moving among other adult rhino, tends to make a mewing whine. This sound, combined with the distress squeak, I was able to imitate and in so doing, particularly with black rhino, call animals towards me.

A wheezy 'hic' is associated with courtship and is usually uttered by a male in his approach to a female. The first time I heard this sound I was sitting in a tree on the Labelweni Ridge, photographing a fractious black rhino and her calf of about three months. Carried to me on the breeze I heard what I at first thought was a distant motor vehicle, almost a throbbing sound, and turned to look in its direction. Across a small watercourse I discerned a white rhino bull in the process of attempting to mount a large cow. I made haste to a good vantage point from which to observe the courting couple and began photographing the action. Awkward and clumsy in his fumbling attempts, the male kept launching himself at the patient cow's rear in his efforts to pull his considerable bulk aboard, and eventually he succeeded in mounting her.

For at least 40 minutes the two rhino alternated between periods of silence with the female standing, head lowered, and the male mounted, head resting on her shoulders, and ejaculating regularly. With each ejaculation he would lift his head and issue a sound somewhere between a wail and a groan, raising and lowering alternately his left and right rear legs. These ejaculations must have taken place every four or five minutes over the entire period during which they remained coupled. It was quite an awe-inspiring performance, and comical too, particularly as the female did not stand motionless but continued walking about at intervals throughout with the male literally in tow, struggling to maintain his position and tottering along on his hind legs.

WHITE RHINO YOUNG

The gestation period of a white rhino is some 16 months. It was my great hope while based in the Umfolozi Game Reserve to photograph a rhino giving birth, but this was not to be and to my knowledge this has never been observed in the wild. Apparently, a short while before the birth the cow retires from her companions, drives off any calf still accompanying her and secludes herself in the densest cover, possibly even timing her parturition to take place during the hours of darkness. The calf is able to walk within 12-24 hours of its birth, and begins grazing when about a week old. It continues to nurse from its mother until well over a year old, and sometimes for up to two years, although the frequency of nursing declines after about 16 months.

White rhino calves suffer very little predation from either lions or hyaenas, the latter known to take a large proportion of young black rhino in East African game parks and believed to be a significant factor in black rhino calf mortality in the Hluhluwe Game Reserve. The fact that the black rhino calf follows its mother while the white runs ahead of her where she can provide protection probably accounts for this.

A rhino calf is the cutest of creatures, almost pig-like in appearance and as inquisitive as a domestic puppy. On two occasions I had calves leave their mothers and wander over to where I was photographing them. Playful and skittish, they would turn and scamper away from time to time, then make a closer approach until I felt it prudent to move before they actually reached out to sniff me and my equipment. In captivity rhino calves quickly become tame and will allow their ears to be scratched and display their investigative nature. Conversely, adult white rhino appear to take a long time to lose their distrust of man and even after months in the bomas at the Natal Parks Board rhino capture unit they were still as wild as the day they were caught.

White rhino are today once again well distributed in the game reserves of southern Africa, thanks to the success of capture and relocation programmes, and appear to be breeding at the near maximum rate of approximately eight to nine per cent a year. In fact their conservation success has been such that they are again available as trophies for hunters with enough money, although to quote author of hunting books Peter Hathaway Capstick (*Death in the Long Grass*, and others), 'the presence of a recently shot white rhino on anybody's wall is to me tantamount to mounting a red banner inscribed "fraud". Sure, there have been some honestly taken white rhinos, but I know of no place where they are available today on a real sporting basis.'

Notes: Reliability of Census:
1 = Total count
2 = Estimated based on rhino survey within last 2 years
3 = Estimated based on rhino survey carried out more than 2 years previously, or recent non-specific survey
4 = Informed guess

Recent trend refers to the past five years.
N/A: Population established too recently for trend to be assessed.
Estimates are those reported and reviewed at the Nyeri Meeting of AERSG, May 1987.

From: African Elephants and Rhinos: Status Survey and Conservation Action Plan; © 1990 International Union for Conservation of Nature and Natural Resources
Compiled by: D.H.M. CUMMING, R.F. DU TOIT and S.N. STUART

Numbers of black and white rhino in South Africa (1987)

AREA	SIZE (KM²)	BLACK RHINO	RELIABILITY OF CENSUS	RECENT TRENDS	WHITE RHINO	RELIABILITY OF CENSUS	RECENT TRENDS
Hluhluwe/Umfolozi G. Reserve	900	220	2	Down	1660	2	Up
Ndumu Game Reserve	100	42	1	Stable	60	2	Up
Mkuzi Game Reserve	251	70	3	Stable	40	3	Up
Itala Game Reserve	297	35	3	N/A	50	3	Up
Eastern Shores G. Reserve	800	10	1	N/A	0		
Weenen Nature Reserve	49	6	1	N/A	14	1	N/A
Kruger National Park	19485	140	2	Up	1200	2	Up
Augrabies National Park	650	5	1	N/A	0		
Addo Elephant National Park	77	17	1	Stable	0		
Andries Vosloo N. Reserve	65	4	1	N/A	0		
Pilanesberg Game Reserve	500	27	2	Up	222	2	Up
Queen Elizabeth Park	Paddock	0			2	1	N/A
Midmar Public Resort N.R.	13	0			3	1	N/A
Chelmsford Public Resort N.R.	40	0			5	1	N/A
Spionkop Public Resort N.R.	30	0			5	1	N/A
Loskop Dam N.R.	148	0			46	2	Stable
Bloemhof Dam N. Reserve	38	0			5	1	N/A
D'Hyala Nature Reserve	80	0			4	1	N/A
Rolfontein Nature Reserve	69	0			6	1	N/A
Thomas Baines N.R.	10	0			3	1	N/A
Kuruman Nature Reserve	9	0			3	1	N/A
Vryburg Nature Reserve	9	0			3	1	N/A
Willem Pretorius G. Reserve	120	0			16	1	N/A
Tussen die Riviere G.R.	220	0			9	1	N/A
Botsalano Game Reserve	58	0			39	2	Up
Tembe Elephant Reserve	300	0			4	1	N/A
Transvaal private land	N/A	1	1		525	2	?
Cape private land	N/A	0			15	2	?
Orange Free State pvt. land	N/A	0			20	2	?
Natal private land	N/A	0			103	1	?
Total		577			4062		

The black rhino

The black rhinoceros (*Diceros bicornis*) was, until recently, the most numerous of all the rhino species, but unprecedented poaching combined with the virtual collapse of law and order through most of Africa during the past two decades has seen their numbers decline by more than 95 per cent, from an estimated 65 000 in 1970 to fewer than 3 500 today. In Kenya alone, despite the large network of game reserves and national parks and a total ban on all hunting, the population plummeted from 20 000 to about 200 during the 1980s, a decline due almost entirely to petty and organized poaching for its horn. In the last five years of the 1980s the surviving population world-wide was more than halved, and the conservation of black rhino became one of the most important wildlife causes in Africa.

Unfortunately for the black rhino its social and breeding habits are not conducive to a rapid revival of its fortunes, even should the poaching be ended. They are by nature solitary animals and the female is receptive only during a brief 24- to 36-hour period of her oestrus cycle.

BLACK RHINO NUMBERS

Formerly widely distributed throughout southern Africa, and indeed through most of Africa south of the Sahara where suitable habitat occurred, black rhino were recorded by Jan van Riebeeck as occurring on the slopes of Table Mountain in 1653; Governor Simon van der Stel almost had his coach toppled by one near Piketberg in the north-western Cape in 1685. Until recent reintroductions, the last black rhino in the Cape (probably of the subspecies *D.b.bicornis*, which still survives in Namibia) was shot in 1853. The last of the line in the Orange Free State was accounted for at Renosterkop near Kroonstad in 1842, and the last in the Transvaal was shot in 1945. Had it not been for a small population safe in the Natal Parks Board reserves of Hluhluwe, Umfolozi and Mkuzi, the black rhino might have been long gone from this part of the subcontinent.

The species may be said to owe its survival in this country to the white rhino, for it was primarily to save this species that the Zululand reserves of Umfolozi and Hluhluwe were proclaimed in 1897. At that time little attention was paid to the black rhino, the species being so common further north in Africa.

By the 1930s it was estimated that only 100-150 black rhino survived in the Hluhluwe-Umfolozi-Corridor complex and Mkuzi further north. Under Natal Parks Board protection the numbers grew to the extent that when Operation Rhino got under way in the '60s it was decided that black rhino too could be relocated to other areas. A major population collapse as a result of certain culling and fire control policies in the '60s and '70s saw the population crash from an estimated 500 to today's official figure

45

of 220. More enlightened policies today appear to have the situation under control, and black rhino numbers once again are increasing. By September 1989 the Natal Parks Board had moved 165 black rhino to other reserves in Natal, and had helped re-establish the species in reserves such as the Kruger National Park, Pilanesberg, and the Andries Vosloo and Sam Knott nature reserves near Grahamstown in the eastern Cape. To date the Natal Parks Board has donated 70 black rhino to the Kruger Park, which now has a population in excess of 160 animals, and 28 to Pilanesberg. Interestingly, biologists estimate the maximum carrying capacity of the Kruger National Park at 3 500 . . . the present world population.

Four subspecies of *Diceros bicornis* are recognized (although this is challenged by some experts), these being *D.b. minor*, the southern African variety; *D.b. bicornis* in Namibia; *D.b. michaeli* in East Africa and an introduced population of 20 in Addo Elephant National Park in the Cape Province; and *D.b. longipes* in Central Africa.

The South African/Namibian population of in excess of 1 050 black rhino is the only population in Africa to have expanded in recent years and is thus of extreme international importance. Of these, some 620 are of the subspecies *D.b. minor* and are spread between nine reserves, including those of Zululand and the Kruger National Park; about 450 *D.b. bicornis* are in five reserves in Namibia and the northern Cape, and there are 20 *D.b. michaeli* in Addo. Zimbabwe has a population of about 1 600 black rhino but because of heavy poaching this population cannot in any way be considered secure. Details of the estimated black rhino populations throughout Africa are given on page 53.

PHYSICAL ASPECTS

Significantly smaller than the white rhino, the black rhino could almost be regarded as the 'sports' version, for in physical appearance it is compact and trim, and longer in the legs than other rhino species. Its outline is noticeably different from that of the white rhino: it holds its shorter, more proportionate head erect and is more hollow-backed than the white. There is no appreciable difference in colour between the two, this generally being a dull brownish-grey in the black rhino – perhaps fractionally darker than the white.

The black rhino is a browser, feeding predominantly on leaves, twigs and branches rather than grazing on grasses like its bigger cousin the white rhino, and to this end is equipped with a 'hooked' upper lip with which it can grasp and manipulate its foodstuff. On close inspection this lip appears almost like a stubby, primitive finger, and is very similar to the tip of an elephant's trunk. This prehensile lip is very noticeable in the field, particularly when the animal is facing you, and is one of the immediately remarkable differences between the black rhino and the white rhino with its heavy, square lips.

Burdened with near-blindness but possessing a superb sense of smell and excellent hearing, the black rhino is ever alert while going about its business. Once its suspicions are aroused very little escapes its attention. Standing perfectly still with ears cocked, nostrils flared and ungainly head swivelling slowly from side to side, tensed and ready to charge – which it does with surprising speed and agility – it scours its surroundings. It may then painstakingly seek out the intruder, stalking in absolute silence, carefully placing one foot at a time, almost human in its concentration. Should you be the object of its attentions, you'd better be ready to climb a tree!

On locating the source of possible danger, the animal will probably charge, head held high until the last moment, and most often pull up in a cloud of dust to inspect the effects of his actions. These lumbering rushes may be repeated several times and are aimed, I believe, at eliciting a reaction from the perceived foe. Short-sighted in the extreme, the average black rhino can probably not identify a motionless object at more than 10 metres. Move, however, and he's like a guided missile zeroing in on a target. During my innumerable encounters with black rhino I found that if I remained still once the animal's attentions had been aroused it would either stalk right up to where I sat (usually safely in the fork of a tree) until close enough to pick up my scent, when it would take fright and flee or, with several loud puffs and snorts, tail tightly curled over its rump, trot off into the distance.

46

A TESTY TEMPERAMENT

One of the major differences between the white and black rhino is in temperament, for where the former is placid and almost pathetically timid, the latter is excitable, belligerent and often ill-tempered in the extreme.

'He is a swinish, cross-grained, ill-favoured, wallowing brute, with a hide like a rasp, an impudent cock of the chin, a roguish leer from out the corner of his eye, a mud-begrimed exterior and a necklace of ticks and horseflies,' wrote Cornwallis Harris of the black rhino. However, if one is prepared to take the risks, the black rhino is certainly one of the easiest of wild animals to photograph in the field, for nine times out of 10 it will either charge you or come mincing closer to investigate your intrusion.

The black rhino's reputation preceded it and when I first embarked on the project that led to this book I was not looking forward to my first encounter. As it turned out, it could not have been nicer. Very early one autumn morning we were out driving along one of the tourist routes, the Sontuli Loop road in Umfolozi. As we rounded a bend we came upon a black rhino casually browsing a small shrub at the roadside. Stopping immediately, I switched off the motor and sat nervously awaiting the charge I was sure would follow. The rhino barely glanced at us and carried on feeding. Because it was still too early to take photographs, we sat watching until the animal turned and began ambling casually up the road directly towards us. There I sat, reverse gear selected, foot on the clutch and hand on the key in the ignition, ready for a quick start and emergency getaway. Sharna, watching the approach through binoculars, whispered, 'He just looks curious, don't start,' and suppressed an amused chuckle at my apparent nervousness. Curious he was . . . he walked straight up to the front of the truck, where he cautiously sniffed at the radiator grille and stared myopically at us over the hood and through the windscreen. Then, with a sigh, he turned aside, plucked a branch of browse from a roadside tree and chewed contentedly. We spent about three hours watching him after that, and eventually he lay down beneath a shrub some four or five metres from where we were parked and went to sleep. We named this animal Vincent, on account of a missing ear, and I worked with him on numerous occasions thereafter, his temperament being far from what I had read and been led to believe.

I subsequently came to the conclusion that black rhino do not deserve their bad reputation and that, treated with caution and respect, they are no more malicious or dangerous than the white species. (Interestingly, all recent injuries recorded in Zululand reserves have been as a result of white rhino encounters.) FC Selous noted from his own personal experiences that 'although a small proportion of animals of this species may have been excessively ill-tempered, and were always ready to charge anything and everything they saw moving, and even to hunt a human being by scent, that was never the character of the great majority of these animals.' He goes on to record, after having researched the matter extensively, that he had been unable to find even one account of a black or white hunter having been killed by a black rhino, although several (such as Oswell and Andersson) were seriously injured.

Belligerent and aggressive specimens certainly do occur though, and there are records of a black rhino in Kenya who charged a steam train twice in succession, eventually retiring much the worse for wear. Sir Alfred E Pease, in *The Book of the Lion*, states: 'Though rhinoceros often charge, I am quite certain that many so-called rhino charges are not charges at all, and, more often as not, when a rhino jumps out of his bed in a thicket with a snort and a rush that is alarming (generally the result more of terror than anger) his only instinct is to get clear of the bother as fast as he can. On such an occasion I have stood stock still at the "ready" without firing, and though he has charged out he has gone careering past without paying me the slightest attention.' He adds, and I heartily agree with him, that you 'do not want to get in the road of a beast which tries to butt over railway trains'.

BLACK RHINO AND MAN

While the black rhino usually will make a fearsome charge on discerning one's presence, the human scent rarely fails to send it blundering blindly, panic-stricken, in the opposite direction. It is able to pick up the human scent even where one has walked some time previously, and in most cases will stand rooted to the spot for a few seconds while it tests the air with nostrils distended, before fleeing.

This terror at the smell of man I was able to put to defensive use, and once I'd become used to the behaviour of these animals I devised a technique for photographing them up close that worked every time. Sitting or lying at ground level, usually behind a natural feature such as a tree trunk, fallen log or shrub, I would 'call' the rhino towards me, either by snapping a few small twigs or imitating the mewing sound uttered by the young of the species when distressed. Sure enough, in most cases the inquisitive black rhino would prick up its ears and begin to advance, usually displaying frank curiosity. The sound of the camera shutter would result in even greater curiosity and draw the animal closer (although a motordrive would invariably frighten it off) and I would continue photographing until the rhino was too close for comfort, usually at about three metres. At that stage I would toss the heavy beanbag which I carried to steady my cameras either directly upwind or on to the snout of the rhino, which never failed to precipitate an immediate retreat. Although I did not do this often as I was reluctant to disturb or frighten the already nervous creatures, it worked every time I tried it when working at getting low-angle close-ups.

One day, on Mbulunga Ridge, I worked my way close to a sleeping black rhino cow and her young male calf and began photographing them at a distance of some 30 metres with a heavy telephoto lens. After some time the calf was aroused by the sound of the camera and rose to his feet, waking his mother in doing so. I carried on photographing them and they immediately zeroed in on my location behind a marula tree and began walking purposefully towards me. When they were about halfway I placed the big lens carefully on the ground behind the tree and pulled myself up into a fork, continuing my photography with another camera and a shorter lens. The pair carried on walking until they stood directly beneath me, heads raised, staring at the curious apparition in the tree. The tip of the cow's snout could not have been more than 30 centimetres from my feet. She then proceeded to rub her nose up and down the tree trunk, on the opposite side from which I'd been leaning, but I could not believe she had failed to pick up my scent. Here was a rhino who was not afraid of man! She continued in this manner for a while; time stood still, so I have no idea how long, until I realized she was moving around the base of the tree and would soon discover my other camera lying there. Fearful she might damage it, I leaned down and dropped the beanbag on her nostrils, and once again my method lived up to my expectations. With a loud snort she wheeled away and, followed by the calf, ran off, stopping about 50 metres away to stare back in my direction before wandering away into the undergrowth.

BLACK RHINO SOCIETY

Black rhino are not gregarious by nature, and are usually found either singly or in pairs (a cow and her adolescent calf), although temporary groups of as many as five or six may be encountered. These aggregations tend to arise out of feeding or drinking conditions rather than social needs. An unusual black rhino bonding was noticed during a black rhino monitoring programme in the Umfolozi-Hluhluwe-Corridor complex in 1989 when a fully grown adult male was seen in the constant company of a relatively young subadult female. No sexual activity was recorded at the initial sighting, and on several subsequent occasions several months apart the two were re-sighted, again with no sexual reasons evident for their companionship. Black rhino bulls are generally solitary, and only briefly pair up with females for breeding purposes.

Encounters between adult black rhino, either male or female, are rarely aggressive and in most cases involve little more than some sparring and vocalizations before both parties settle down or go their separate ways. The following encounter seems typical. One morning I was observing a cow and her young calf, a male of about a year, lying in a dust wallow when I noticed another pair of black rhino approaching. The second pair also consisted of a cow with a male calf, although he was slightly larger than the first calf, probably about three years old. As they neared the first two, these stood up, and there was a lot of blowing and snorting for some time. All four rhino then cautiously approached each other, heads outstretched, and touched noses. The two young males sparred with each other for a while before they broke apart and rejoined their mothers, who by then had wandered about 10 metres apart. The first pair walked into the shade of a nearby tree while the newcomers took up occupancy of the wallow, settling down and going to sleep. After watching for a few minutes, the first pair also lay down and resumed their slumbers.

Black rhino are not territorial to the extent of white rhino, and move over wide areas in search of food and water throughout the year. However, when browse, water and wallows are readily available they appear to develop fairly limited home ranges, although these can be as large as 100 square kilometres. While clashes between adult males are rare, in areas where population densities are high and competition for food and water is at a premium, young adults are frequently severely and sometimes fatally injured by other rhino defending their home ranges. This has led to conservation authorities such as the Natal Parks Board monitoring population densities and capturing subadult animals for relocation to reserves in other areas.

Violent clashes between adult males also occur in competition over breeding females, and mortal injuries are not uncommon, while 'territorial' disputes between old males and younger rivals occasionally take place. Bulls are very aggressive towards young rhino, particularly when a cow is in oestrus, and the previous season's calf is in constant danger of being killed if it remains too close to its mother when a bull is attempting to mate with her. Conversely, the cows are very protective, and frequently attack and injure or drive off other black rhino if they appear aggressive towards their offspring.

Most rhino will drink on a daily basis when water is available, but can survive for three or four days without it, such as in the case of the desert black rhino (*D. b. bicornis*) of Namibia's Kaokoveld. Most feeding and drinking takes place through the night and in the early morning and late afternoon, with most of the midday hours spent asleep.

During the winter months black rhino appear to prefer resting in the sun and can often be found fast asleep in a sunny clearing, while the white rhino has a preference for shade. Like the white rhino, the black appears to enjoy nothing more than a muddy wallow followed by a scratch at a rubbing post. In summer they can often be observed sleeping for hours immersed in temporary rainwater pans and vleis. Unlike the white rhino, however, which appears to be constantly alert at such times, the black rhino seems to drift into a kind of 'deep sleep mode' from which it is often difficult to rouse it.

Ranger Tom Yule and I encountered this 'sleep mode', as we termed it, on quite a few occasions and once had two black rhino carry on sleeping while we literally demolished a dead tree, shouted and clapped hands about 40 metres away. These rhino eventually awoke of their own accord, yawned, stood and stretched, then ambled off and began browsing on some choice *Acacia karroo* shoots without so much as a glance in our direction. On another occasion we crawled across the open to a small tree about 10-15 metres from where a large black rhino bull lay sleeping. Tom climbed into the tree and I sat at its base, ready to climb quickly if necessary. We made a few noises and the rhino awoke, raised its head and peered at us quite nonchalantly. Twice he stood up and wandered towards us to investigate the source of the strange noises, as well as the motions we were making in an attempt to attract his attention, but would not come close. On both occasions, after looking quite puzzled – I'm sure he would have scratched his head had he been able – he lay down and dropped off to sleep again. After further futile attempts to rouse him we left him in peace – and nicknamed him Dozy!

I encountered this apparent disinterest on awakening on frequent other occasions, once to such an extent that I became concerned that the animal was hurt or ill and unable to rise. I had been out walking early one morning and was heading back to camp at a brisk pace, not paying much attention to my surroundings, when I breasted a rise and found right before me a sleeping black rhino. A few redbilled oxpeckers were in attendance and immediately gave the alarm, at which the rhino raised his head, albeit lethargically. I ran to a tree, but the rhino showed no sign of alarm or intention of rising, so I moved forward, zigzagging from tree to tree until I was less than 10 paces from him. Still the rhino lay unmoving, merely following my movements with his ears and eyes. By then I was certain he was injured, for from my vantage point it appeared that his right rear leg was lying awkwardly. Wanting to be certain before rushing off to summon the reserve veterinarian, I tossed a stone at the animal. Apart from a small snort when the stone landed next to him and rolled away, there was no reaction. I picked up a bigger stone, about the size and shape of a cricket ball, and rolled it down the slope. It hit him right on the nose. This, at last, galvanized him into action and he sprang to his feet without a problem and ran off down the slope.

PREDICTABILITY

However, this should not give you the idea that the black rhino is a harmless creature. Perhaps their saving grace, for man, is their predictability – 99 times out of a hundred they are likely to charge, though I believe that many of these 'charges' are merely curious advances, or threatening rushes designed to provoke intruders into revealing their presence. The best advice I can give anyone unfortunate enough to be charged by a black rhino is to climb a tree . . . if it is nearby. If you're trapped out in the open and your nerves can stand it, remain motionless, preferably flat on the ground, and the rhino is unlikely to be able to locate you. If you run away you are likely to be chased, and a charging black rhino can attain speeds of 40-50 kilometres per hour and is undeterred by obstacles such as thornscrub and brush.

Dr Peter Rogers, a vet with the Natal Parks Board in Zululand, was once saved from serious injury when he fell while fleeing from an angry black rhino that had been gaining on him with every step. Once down he remained motionless (frozen with terror!) and the rhino, unable to locate him, was eventually distracted by a person further away, allowing the fortunate doctor to make good his escape. My friend Vincent, the one-eared black rhino, gave me a good scare one day after I'd been photographing him for several hours and had relaxed my guard a bit too much. Normally placid and approachable, he suddenly took exception to my proximity and charged straight for me. I had barely hoisted myself into a not particularly suitable tree when he hit the trunk with a thud only a few centimetres from my lowest extremity. As I struggled to pull myself higher he took a vicious swipe with his horn and bark went flying. My shouted expletives had little effect on him and it was only once I'd managed to climb a few feet higher that he lost interest and charged off into the nearest thicket, huffing and puffing like a steam train.

The tree-climbing ability one develops when working in rhino country is remarkable. I came to judge a tree by no factor other than its 'climbability', for example marulas were 'good trees' while several of the excessively thorny acacias were 'bad trees' – not that thorns make much difference when you are fleeing from an angry rhino.

BLACK RHINO AND THEIR ENEMIES

Many black rhino have raw, bleeding lesions on their sides and chests, caused by the filariform parasitic worm *Stephanofilaria dinniki*. These lesions, common in black rhino in East Africa, are also carried by the animals in Zululand. Although the ulcerative sores, which vary in size from animal to animal depending on the animal's age and maturity, look extremely ugly and painful they appear to cause the black rhino no ill effects. They can be quite useful in estimating the age of a black rhino, particularly that of the younger animals, as lesions appear only after the rhino reaches a certain age, and their distribution on the rhino's body changes with time.

All rhino are victims of the same major predator – man – and adult black rhino suffer little predation from other animals, although lions have been known to kill adults on rare occasions. Lions, and spotted hyaenas in particular, do however have a serious effect on black rhino calf survival rates and it has been proposed that in areas where black rhino populations and breeding rates need to be increased it may be necessary to eliminate these predators.

During our time spent in Botswana several years ago one of the few rhino left in that country caused much excitement near a popular game lodge when one day it appeared with a calf in tow. The next day, however, all that was left of the calf was a bloody carcass, and an extremely satisfied-looking lion was seen nearby. In Tanzania researcher Hans Kruuk discovered that spotted hyaenas play a major role in black rhino infant mortality. He noted that the hyaenas preferentially grab black rhino calves by the ears, which could account for the number of black rhino I encountered missing either one or both ears.

BREEDING AND BIRTH RATES

Black rhino breed throughout the year, having no specific breeding season. The gestation period is 15-16 months. Like the white rhino, and indeed all of the species, the male appears to have great staying power and copulation can last as long as an hour with regular ejaculations throughout. It is thought that this sexual stamina gave rise to the belief in rhino horn as an aphrodisiac.

Black rhino birth rates are currently the subject of some concern, particularly with the recent losses due to poaching: it appears that a rhino gives birth every three to five years. Wild rhino do not breed as fast as their physiology would allow, probably because cows breed again only when an existing calf is able to fend for itself. A rhino cow should be able to produce a calf every 22 months and, should captive breeding programmes be instituted, it may be possible to double current birth rates. Dr Martin Brooks, South African representative of the IUCN's African Elephant and Rhino Specialist Group and senior researcher with the Natal Parks Board, suggests that the aim of increasing South Africa's black rhino population from 650 to 2 000 could succeed 'if we can increase current birth rates to about eight per cent. At that rate we'll have 2 000 *D.b. minor* within about 14 years.'

As with the white rhino, the black rhino cow hides in dense undergrowth to give birth. The calf weighs 25-40 kilograms, is capable of walking within about 10 minutes of birth, and nurses for well over a year. The calf stays with its mother until the next one is born, and even then may rejoin the cow and her calf once the new calf is a few months old. Black rhino reach sexual maturity at about six or seven years, and may live for as long as 60 years, although 45 is the accepted average.

A PASSION FOR BLACK RHINO

Prior to my stay in the Umfolozi Game Reserve elephants were my favourite photographic subjects, for they show interesting behaviour, are relatively easy to approach on foot, and the element of danger involved adds interest and excitement. However, after working with rhino for a year I must confess that the *bhejane* (Zulu for black rhino) has captured my affections. The fact that, like the elephant, he can and will kill you given the chance adds spice to the encounter. Their behavioural characteristics and activities are very different from those of elephants, certainly, and it is perhaps something intangible that makes them special. I know these feelings are shared by everyone who has worked closely with black rhino, and to hear a group of *bhejane* enthusiasts regaling each other with accounts of their exploits is to listen to fanatics.

Who other than a fanatic (and all wildlife photographers are of necessity fanatics) would spend five hours in a bitter wind sitting up a tree, quietly waiting for a couple of sleeping rhino to awaken and go about their business?

It was the middle of July and we had left camp in the predawn darkness to head for Manzimhlope Valley deep in the Corridor, where we had seen several black rhino the day before. The sun was sliding over the eastern hills when we located our first rhino of the day, a black cow and her calf. I loaded my camera pack and set off on foot, but after an hour returned to the vehicle having had little success. Driving to a high point we scoured the surrounding hills and valleys with binoculars. Soon we spotted another black rhino cow with a calf, and headed down the track in their direction. As we neared them I saw another group of three black rhino browsing under some trees. Again I set off on foot, making my way across the open hillside but through grass that was chest-high in places. I was angling uphill towards where I'd seen the three under the trees when I almost walked into a black rhino cow and her 30-month-old calf asleep in the grass. I beat a hasty retreat and climbed into a flimsy, fire-blackened acacia in order to get a better view. I made quite a racket climbing the tree, cracking dead branches underfoot. Both rhino scrambled to their feet and peered disconcertedly in my direction, although where I was about 40 metres away they would not have been able to see anything. Soon they relaxed, lay down and resumed their sleep.

Deciding the acacia was not suitable – the light was coming from the wrong angle and the tree was swaying in the strong south-westerly wind that had come up – I decided to make an attempt at a 'good tree' I could see, about 20 metres on the far side of where the two rhino lay sleeping. I could also make out the other three black rhino browsing among the trees further up the hillside, as well as another white rhino and its calf and several buffalo. I would have to move very carefully if I were to reach my chosen tree without spooking the other animals in the vicinity, which was sure to set them all running and so alarm my targetted sleeping duo.

After a nervous approach which took some 30 minutes I saw my first choice of tree was not entirely suitable, and moved towards another, more climbable tree, even closer to where the two rhino lay sleeping peacefully. Eventually I reached the tree, a half-dead umbrella thorn, and with heart pounding clambered into it, again quite noisily, causing dead branches to break and crash to the ground. The rhino, now only some 15 paces from me, jumped up at the disturbance, and squinted myopically in my direction. I sat still and silent, and they soon seemed satisfied that I presented no threat and, without showing any further curiosity, lay down again and dropped off to sleep. I proceeded to photograph them and even the sound of the camera failed to arouse their interest. Realizing I could be in for a long wait, I cleared a few dead branches from around me and made myself comfortable.

As the hours crept by I debated awakening the rhino, but decided I'd rather let them rise in their own time in the hope they would then go about their normal activities without worrying about my presence. After about three hours the rhino stood up, moved closer to my tree and lay down again, this time on their opposite flanks. The wind continued to blow, and in my exposed position it took all my energy to prevent my teeth from chattering so loudly I'd disturb the animals. Two crows flew in, and after squawking loudly at me from a treetop, they fluttered down and landed on the adult rhino's flank. There, they marched boldly up and down, pecking at ticks and even tearing chunks of flesh from the raw and bloody lesions on her side, at which the rhino would only shudder and snort.

The crows left and I resumed my solitary vigil. Far in the distance I could make out buildings outside the reserve, and from time to time a vehicle passed by on a road far away. There was something unreal about being perched in a tree, two black rhino sleeping about 10 metres away, a white rhino cow and her calf about 50 metres to the rear and another three black rhino some 100 metres further up the hillside, and in the distance to see 'civilization'. I whiled away the time wondering at the perplexities of conservation, and the threats to these animals in the future. I thought about the fact that the reality of rural poverty is perhaps the greatest threat to wildlife today, that impoverished communities, while perhaps supporting the concepts of conservation, do not have the economic leeway to support it in practice. To these people, the destruction of wildlife, plants as well as game, is often a necessity of survival. A rhino horn is equivalent to a year's wages, or more, for many rural Africans.

My reverie was eventually broken by signs of life down below. The adult cow stood and scratched her rump against a nearby tree. The calf, yawning, seemed reluctant to move. Taking advantage of her offspring's still-prone position, the cow walked over and, straddling the calf, proceeded to give her belly a good rub on its back. They both then wandered to some scrub and began to browse. My cameras were working overtime and the rhino, although glancing in my direction now and then, remained unperturbed. Their browsing brought them ever closer, and soon they stood some five metres from me, staring intently as I changed position to alter my camera angle. Then they moved towards and past me on the downwind side of the tree.

Suddenly they were in my wind, and both froze, nostrils flared. I carried on clicking away, moving between shots. The rhino looked at me in a cursory way, and then looked beyond me, further upwind, obviously discounting the strange thing in the tree as the man they could smell. After a while they moved back upwind of me, appearing not to want to cross the scent of man. The cow seemed agitated, but the calf lay down again.

This had a calming effect on the cow, and soon she resumed feeding, joined by junior a short while later.

Once again, the pair attempted to move downwind of me, caught my scent and moved back. I climbed out of the tree and squatted beside the trunk to get a lower-angle viewpoint, and still the rhino ignored me. After several further attempts to walk downwind of me the rhino decided to circle around upwind. I followed them and found them standing some way off, staring back in the direction from which they'd come. Every now and again the cow would make short charging rushes at nothing in particular, then stop suddenly and listen intently. It was an action very obviously designed to put anything to flight, so she could hear and possibly see it when it moved.

Bidding them farewell, I returned to where Sharna waited with the vehicle, spiritually enriched by my close encounter of a special kind.

Numbers of black rhino in African countries 1980-1990

(Estimates by the African Elephant and Rhino Specialist Group of the IUCN.)

COUNTRY	1980	1984	1986	1987	1990
Zimbabwe	1 400	1 680	1 625	1 775	1 600
South Africa	630	640	548	572	650
Namibia	300	400	440	440	450
Kenya	1 500	550	381	511	200
Tanzania	3 795	3 130	400	255	?
Zambia	2 750	1 650	190	95	40
Central African Republic	3 000	170	150	?	?
The Cameroon	110	110	60	30	?
Mozambique	250	130	130	?	200?
Sudan	300	100	20	?	?
Somalia	300	90	0	0	0
Angola	300	90	50	?	?
Malawi	40	20	25	20+	?
Rwanda	30	15	20	15	?
Botswana	30	10	10	2	2
Ethiopia	30	10	?	2	?
Chad	25	5	0	0	0
Uganda	5	0	0	0	0
Swaziland	0	0	0	6	6

There are some 190 black rhino in 71 zoo populations around the world. These are primarily of the East African subspecies *D.b. michaeli*. A further small breeding group of *D.b. minor* from Zululand exists in Texas, USA. (Scientists maintain that populations of substantially less than 500 animals are not genetically or ecologically viable.)

The Indian rhino

The great one-horned rhino, or Indian rhino (*Rhinoceros unicornis*), is perhaps the most prehistoric-looking of all the rhino, with its heavily folded skin studded with rivet-like tubercules giving the appearance of armour-plating. Immortalized by German artist Albrecht Dürer almost five centuries ago in drawings and woodcuts based on descriptions of a specimen that had been sent by an Indian ruler as a gift to King Manuel of Portugal, its armoured appearance led to the belief, common until early this century, that the animal was bulletproof. (A British soldier in India once shot and killed the regimental mascot, an Indian rhino, to test this belief!)

PHYSICAL DIMENSIONS AND SOCIAL STRUCTURE

Massive and thickset, the Indian rhino is slightly smaller than the white rhino, though some specimens stand taller at the shoulder. Unlike both African species, the Indian rhino has long pointed incisor teeth which it frequently bares in threat displays and will use effectively in fighting. It carries only one horn, which is far shorter and less pointed than those of the African rhino. Feeding mainly at night, the Indian rhino is both a grazer and a browser, with some 80 per cent of its diet being made up of grass and the balance of bamboo shoots, leaves, twigs, water hyacinth and even agricultural crops where these are available. Like the other rhino species, it loves water and wallowing, and groups of Indian rhino are often observed wallowing together, the waterhole being treated as a social meeting place where the presence of others is tolerated. The Indian rhino is most frequently found in association with swamps surrounded by dense forest, and is known to swim quite readily.

Unsociable at the best of times, this species is known for its irascibility and violent clashes between members of the species are frequent, particularly between males competing over a breeding cow. (In Nepal, elephants used to transport tourist into wildlife areas are specially trained to stand in the face of charging rhino, for the occurrence is not rare.)

The Indian rhino is not territorial and does not use the urine-spraying technique of scent-marking common in the white and black rhino, although it does make use of middens. These, however, appear not to have any territorial significance and are probably used merely to advise other rhino of a rhino's presence in the area – a kind of rhino social directory.

BREEDING

Females become sexually mature at six or seven years, at which stage they will begin to attract the attentions of dominant bulls and other males in the vicinity. Courtship is frequently marked by violence, and when a male makes his initial approaches to a cow, even when she is in oestrus, she will attempt to drive him off with charges and slashes of her incisors. Horn-to-horn sparring usually ensues, an encounter from which the female will eventually flee with the male in hot pursuit, often for several kilometres. On catching up with her, the male will resume the head-to-head position, and both animals will roar and pant as they shove each other back and forth with vicious lunges, their incisors displayed. These activities may take some time, and are interspersed with regular rest periods, but it is always the male who resumes the battle until the cow, exhausted, lies down in submission. The male then either stands astride her, biting victoriously at the air, or lies down close beside her, his aggression abated.

Prior to mating the male will rest his head on the cow's rump, keeping it there even should the cow walk around, in the same manner as both the black and white rhino of Africa. As can be expected with an animal of this size, mounting is an awkward action and can take a long time to achieve, with the male launching himself forward on his hind legs while trying to get his forefeet on to the female's back. Once mounted, his troubles have not ended, for he must endeavour to remain there while the female continues about her business, often walking about feeding quite nonchalantly as he shuffles along behind. Copulation may last as long as an hour and, as with the African varieties and no doubt the Javan and Sumatran as well, includes multiple ejaculations.

A single calf is born after a gestation period of about 16 months; although twins have been recorded these must be considered extremely rare.

CONSERVATION

The Indian rhino is currently well protected in both India and Nepal, where a total of some 2 000 is increasing at more than five per cent a year, a factor influenced by both good protection and the lack of organized poaching. Their biggest threat at present, as with wildlife everywhere, is the rapidly increasing human population, and in spite of the stability of the population, the animal is still regarded as seriously endangered.

The largest population is that existing in the Kaziranga National Park in India, where there are in excess of 1 000 of the species. A further population has been relocated to the Dudhwa National Park in the same country, with reported success. Enlightened conservation policies in Nepal, and the fact that rhino are protected by royal edict, have resulted in rhino conservation in the country being a great success, with current population estimates of about 500 animals for the Royal Bardia and Chitawan national parks and their surrounds. The fact that the Royal Nepalese Army patrols the park twice daily, while the forestry department patrols outside their borders, probably contributes in no uncertain way to the country's success in all but eliminating poaching.

Because certain rhino products are regarded as important to the local people for certain ceremonial and medicinal purposes, any rhino that dies in the park is made available to the local populace. This has further reduced the incidence of poaching, as these products are made freely available at reasonable prices – and perhaps therein lies a valuable lesson for Western wildlife managers.

The Javan rhino

The lesser one-horned Asian rhino, or Javan rhino (*Rhinoceros sondaicus*), is smaller than the Indian rhino although similar to it in many respects: it has the same armoured appearance but lacks the heavy folds of skin and the 'rivetted' appearance of the Indian rhino.

At one stage during the last century Javan rhino were so numerous and considered to be such pests that a bounty was offered for their deaths. Obviously the policy was successful: previously widely distributed from India throughout south-east Asia, the Javan rhino was hunted almost to extinction; today there remain only some 50 animals in the Ujung Kulon National Park in Java and a recently discovered group of about 15 in a remote area in Vietnam. The last two specimens in Burma were 'collected' for the British Museum in 1920, while the last surviving Javan rhino in Malaya was shot – also for a museum – in 1932. The species was declared extinct in Sumatra in the mid-1940s.

The Javan rhino has never been successfully studied in the wild, despite a number of attempts by scientists of various nationalities. As a result, very little is known about the species.

Only the male possesses a horn, this being small and rounded, while the female carries little more than a raised knob. The Javan rhino has a scaly, segmented appearance similar to that of an armadillo. Forest dwellers, they are browsers with a prehensile upper lip similar to that of the black rhino. They are believed to be territorial and mark their territories by urine-spraying, but do not make use of middens.

Although there is a limited threat from poaching, no doubt due to the difficulty in finding even a single animal, the species is in imminent danger of extinction. Attempts to save it are being hampered by a very slow birth rate. Javan conservation authorities, funded by international bodies such as the World Wide Fund for Nature (WWF), are attempting to capture part of the remaining population for relocation to an isolated island sanctuary where there would be less threat from poaching and habitat destruction, as well as to develop a captive breeding programme to reinforce the species in the wild.

The Sumatran rhino

The Asian two-horned rhino, or Sumatran rhino (*Dicerorhinus sumatrensis*) is the smallest of all the species, and probably also the least evolved. Covered with the dense coat of dark hair that has given it the name of 'buffalo rhino' among local hunters, it is not all that different in appearance from the prehistoric rhino, such as the woolly rhinoceros, which disappeared during the Ice Age of some 15 000-20 000 years ago.

The Sumatran rhino was widely distributed until the turn of the century throughout Sumatra, Borneo, Malaya, Burma, Thailand, Laos, Vietnam, Cambodia, Bengal and Assam, with its range overlapping that of the Javan rhino except in Java itself. The decline of the species can be attributed to both legal and illegal hunting (like the two other Asian rhino, the Sumatran species has been killed for thousands of years to satisfy the demand for its horn for medicinal purposes), as well as loss of habitat due to the clearing of tropical forests.

The Sumatran rhino is sparsely scattered through reserves in Indonesia, Malaysia and Burma, and possibly Thailand. The total world population is estimated at between 400 and 900.

The species has not been studied successfully in the wild, and only two living specimens exist in zoos outside of its homeland. Most of what is known about it is derived from native hearsay, along with the notes and records of early explorers and hunters, combined with studies of captive animals in recent years. It is a forest dweller and has a prehensile upper lip like its black and Javan cousins, enabling it to feed on leaves, twigs, fruit and cane shoots. It will frequently 'walk down' small trees, in much the same manner as the black and Javan rhino, in order to reach the new shoots and leaves at the crown.

Although close to extinction, the Sumatran rhino may be facing a brighter future following research that has shown the species should be able to survive in commercial forests, providing logging is selective and certain allowances are made for the animals. A captive breeding centre in the Tabin Reserve in Sabah (formerly North Borneo) has plans to reintroduce captive-bred animals into other areas where they previously occurred. There are also proposals to develop captive breeding programmes in England and America, where there is appreciable expertise and the resources that can be utilized to expedite the exercise. It is hoped to develop a captive 'gene pool' of 150 Sumatran rhino in zoos around the world, established from 20 founders from the wild.

57

Rhino: where to see them

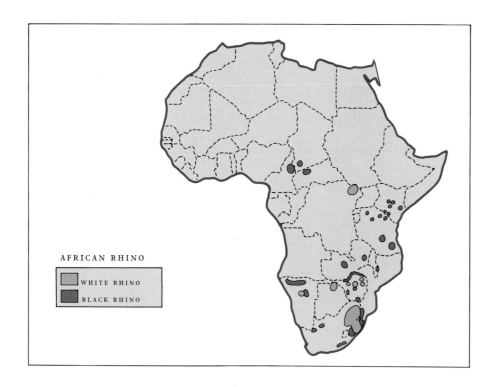

AFRICAN RHINO

WHITE RHINO

BLACK RHINO

Watching rhino in the wild is to take a peek back into primordial time, for there are few creatures on earth that can evoke such awe by their prehistoric presence. Unfortunately, by their very nature, as well as the inordinate pressures exerted by man and their subsequent withdrawal into the remotest regions, rhino-watching is not the easiest of pastimes.

The chances of seeing either the Sumatran or the Javan rhino in the wild are negligible. However, for the determined, the most likely venues are the Gunung Leuser National Park or the Tabin Reserve in Sabah for the former, and the Ujung Kulon National Park in Java for the latter.

Indian rhino are far more plentiful and thus relatively easily seen in their natural state, and safari operations such as the famed Tree Tops Lodge in Nepal offer special rhino-viewing outings for the adventurous, atop trained elephants. The best rhino-watching spots for this species are undoubtedly the Chitawan National Park in Nepal and the Kaziranga National Park in Assam Province, India, which has an estimated 1 000 animals. The Dudhwa National Park, also in India, has a smaller population.

Black rhino were not so long ago frequently sighted in the major tourist reserves of East Africa, with vast populations of the species occurring in Tsavo, Amboseli and on the plains of the Maasai Mara in Kenya, as well as in Tanzania's Serengeti and Selous national parks, and in Ngorongoro Crater. Today the black rhino has been all but eliminated by poaching in Tanzania, and official estimates put the number in Kenya at not many more than 200. Kenyan wildlife authorities have built specially protected stockades for the species in national parks such as Tsavo, Aberdare Forest, Nakuru, Meru and Amboseli, and it is here that one is most likely to see black rhino when in Kenya. The private Solio, Ol Joli, Laikipia and Lewa Downs game ranches also have small populations.

Africa's largest population of black rhino (1 600+) occurs at present in Zimbabwe but is coming under increasing poaching pressure. As a result the animals, which occur primarily in the Zambezi Valley and Sebungwe district, are extremely shy and rarely seen by tourists on the beaten track. The dense vegetation in this area compounds the difficulty in seeing them, but visitors to Mana Pools National Park should have some success. Zimbabwe's Hwange National Park has a growing population of both black (300+) and white (100+) rhino and these may be observed at the park's watering holes, particularly at those where night-viewing is permitted (both black and white species generally drink at night). Zimbabwean authorities have relocated almost 300 black rhino to other unspecified parks and private reserves in the midlands, where they will be safer from poachers from the north.

Zambia's Luangwa Valley, for so long a choice rhino area and one of the best places to see these animals in the wild, has also fallen victim to unprecedented poaching. In the under-staffed and under-financed parks numbers have declined to a recent estimate of about 40, so chances of encountering rhino there must now be rated as very slim.

Namibia's black rhino population, particularly those protected within the Etosha National Park (population 350+), is perhaps among the most easily seen of all, for these animals frequently come to drink at night at the floodlit watering hole at Okaukuejo camp. Special tours designed to cater for those wishing to catch a glimpse of the unique desert-dwelling rhino and elephant of the Kaokoveld (rhino population 80+) are also available, although with these animals so widely distributed these is no guarantee of success. Black rhino have been relocated to the new Waterberg Plateau Park (population 25), where the possibility of seeing these animals is fair.

INDIAN RHINO

JAVAN RHINO

SUMATRAN RHINO

South Africa's extensive array of national parks, provincial reserves and private game farms and reserves offers perhaps Africa's greatest rhino-watching opportunities today.

The white rhino has been relocated to both state-owned and privately owned land throughout the country, and can be seen with relative ease in places such as the Pilanesberg National Park in Bophuthatswana, the Kruger National Park, and the famous 'rhino reserves' of Umfolozi, Hluhluwe and Mkuzi in Zululand. Privately owned game reserves such as Sabi Sand, Timbavati, Umbabat and Tshukudu, all in the north-eastern Transvaal, and Ubizane and Nyala Trails in Natal, have reintroduced white rhino and can virtually guarantee you a sighting of them during a short stay.

The Kruger Park's rhino population is currently undergoing major expansions and the prognosis for the animal in this reserve appears to be excellent. There are already well over 1 200 white rhino here, and the black rhino population (in excess of 160 animals) is also doing well. However, as the Kruger Park covers an enormous area the best opportunity of seeing rhino here falls to those prepared to undertake a foot trail in the company of a trained and armed game ranger, for which advance reservations are essential.

Umfolozi, Hluhluwe and Mkuzi game reserves offer probably the best rhino-viewing in the world, particularly where the white rhino is concerned. The population of the Umfolozi-Hluhluwe-Corridor complex is so high (approaching 2 000) that it is virtually impossible to avoid seeing these animals, while at Mkuzi several excellent game-viewing hides at watering holes provide superb viewing opportunities. The newly created Itala Game Reserve, also in Natal, has a growing population of relocated rhino, white and black, and will also provide good opportunities for rhino watching.

Black rhino are by nature solitary and elusive, and their habitat makes them difficult to observe in the wild. Even though the Umfolozi-Hluhluwe-Corridor complex has a high population density of this species (220-250) they are by no means easy to find. Perhaps the best chance one would have of encountering black rhino here is on foot on a guided walk, or during one of the wilderness trails run by the Natal Parks Board and Wilderness Leadership School through the Umfolozi wilderness area, particularly in the spring months when the grass is short after the winter burns.

Falling under the aegis of the National Parks Board of South Africa are three reserves in the Cape Province – Addo

Elephant, Vaalbos and Augrabies Falls national parks. The Addo Elephant National Park has South Africa's sole population of *D.b. michaeli*, the East African subspecies, which was relocated here in 1960 and 1961, while the other two parks have small populations of *D.b. bicornis*, the Namibian subspecies.

Also in the Cape, the Andries Vosloo and adjoining Sam Knott nature reserves have in recent years introduced black rhino from Zululand. The population in these reserves today numbers nine.

Swaziland's network of small game reserves provides limited rhino-viewing opportunities, primarily because of extremely dense vegetation, although the Hlane National Park in the east of the country has a sizeable white rhino population. Mlilwane Game Sanctuary, near Mbabane, has a small group of white rhino that are remarkable for their tameness. A group of six black rhino, reintroduced from Zimbabwe, is located on a private game reserve, Mkhaya, controlled by conservationist Ted Reilly. He hopes to add a further six black rhino to this group in the near future, for the habitat at Mkhaya has been assessed by international black rhino consultant Peter Jenkins, advisor to the Kenyan wildlife authorities, as capable of supporting at least 100 of these animals.

Numbers of black and white rhino in southern Africa (other than South Africa) (1987)

AREA	SIZE (KM²)	BLACK RHINO	RELIABILITY OF CENSUS	RECENT TRENDS	WHITE RHINO	RELIABILITY OF CENSUS	RECENT TRENDS
Angola		No data			0		
Botswana							
Moremi and Chobe areas	15380	<10	4	?	100-150	4	?
Malawi							
Kasungu National Park	2316	20	3	Stable	0		
Mwabvi Game Reserve	340	5	4	?	0		
Total		25			0		
Mozambique		v. low nbr		Down	0		Recently extinct
Namibia							
Etosha National Park	22270	350	3	Stable	0		
Damaraland	13000	5-8	2	Stable	0		
Kaokoland	3500	85-100	2	Up	0		
Waterberg National Park	400	0			28	2	Up
Private land	N/A	0			35	2	Down?
Total		440-458			63		
Swaziland					60-100	4	Down?
Zambia							
Kafue National Park	22400	20	4	Down	0		
Mweru-Wantipa National Park	3134	5	4	?	0		
Luangwa South N.P.	9050	50	3	Stable?	0		
Chindini Hills GMA	?	>6	3	Down	0		
Lukusuzi National Park	2720	5	4	Down	0		
Lumimba GMA	4500	>10	4	Down	0		
Luano/W. Petauke GMAs	13000	10	4	Down	0		
Livingstone Game Park	10	0			6	1	Down
Total		>106			6		
Zimbabwe							
Zambezi Valley	11000	750	3	Down	0		
Sebungwe Region	5000	650	3	Stable/Up	0		
Hwange/Matetsi	18400	>260	3	Stable/Up	110	3	?
Gonarezhou National Park	3900	75	3	Down	0		
Matopos National Park	432	5	1	N/A	28	1	Stable
Private ranches	N/A	14	1	N/A	26	1	Stable
Lake Kyle Recreation Park	90	0			30	3	Stable
Lake McIlwaine Rec. Park	61	0			8	1	Stable
Ngamo/Sikumi Forest Land	930	0			4	1	N/A
Cecil Kop Reserve		0			2	1	N/A
Total		>1754			208		

Numbers of black and white rhino in West, Central and East Africa (1987)

AREA	SIZE (KM²)	BLACK RHINO	RELIABILITY OF CENSUS	RECENT TRENDS	WHITE RHINO	RELIABILITY OF CENSUS	RECENT TRENDS
Cameroon/Chad	5000	30	4	Down	0		
Central African Republic	N/A	10	4	Down	0		
Ethiopia/Somalia	N/A	?			0		
Kenya							
Amboseli N.P. and surrounds	800	10	1	Stable	0		
Nairobi National Park	117	>32	2	Stable	0		
Aberdare National Park	766	60	4	?	0		
Masai Mara National Reserve	1510	19	1	Down	0		
Meru National Park	870	>5	3	Down	6	1	Stable
Tsavo National Park	20200	150	4	Down	0		
Nakuru National Park	140	2	1	N/A	0		
Marsabit N.R.	140	5	4	Down	0		
Tana River	N/A	6	3	Down	0		
Ngeng Valley	N/A	18	2	Down	0		
North Horr	N/A	3	3	Down	0		
Nguruman Escarpment	N/A	5	3	Down	0		
Laikipia Ranch	350	47	1	Stable/Up	0		
Lewa Downs Ranch	20	11	1	N/A	1	1	N/A
Ol Jogi Ranch		7	1	N/A	0		
Solio Ranch	52	91	1	Up	40	1	Up
Mount Kenya National Park	700	50	4	?	0		
Total		>521			47		
Rwanda							
Akagera National Park	2500	15	4	Stable?	0		
Sudan							
Badingeru G.R.	5000	3	1	Down	0		
Tanzania							
Selous Game Reserve	55000	200	3	Down	0		
Lake Manyara National Park	320	5	4	Down	0		
Ngorongoro Conservation Area	8288	20-30	3	Down	0		
Ruaha N.P./Rungwa G.R.	27216	10	4	Down	0		
Serengeti N.P./Maswa G.R.	14763	<10	4	Down	0		
Rubondo National Park	457	20-30	4	Stable?	0		
Total		265-285			0		
Zaïre							
Garamba National Park	4900	0			22	1	Up
Continental totals		c. 3800			4568-4658		

Notes: Reliability of Census:
1 = Total count
2 = Estimated based on rhino survey within last 2 years
3 = Estimated based on rhino survey carried out more than 2 years previously, or recent non-specific survey
4 = Informed guess

Recent trend refers to the past five years. N/A: Population established too recently for trend to be assessed.
Estimates are those reported and reviewed at the Nyeri Meeting of AERSG, May 1987.

From: African Elephants and Rhinos: Status Survey and Conservation Action Plan; © 1990 International Union for Conservation of Nature and Natural Resources
Compiled by: D.H.M. CUMMING, R.F. DU TOIT and S.N. STUART

Poaching and the rhino horn trade

*'Despite worldwide efforts to safeguard the wildlife of Africa
its survival is in jeopardy simply because its future lies in the hands
of those who threaten it — human beings.'*
PETER BEARD   *The End of The Game*

It is ironic that the rhino's horn, which evolved for its protection, should become its Achilles' heel, the cause of its being mercilessly hunted to the brink of extinction by poachers throughout its historic and present range. It is tragic too that this magnificent creature should now be nearing extermination because of the greed and misguided traditional beliefs of peoples who have more than likely never even seen a picture of a rhinoceros, let alone one in a zoo or in the wild. The perilous situation of both the Javan and Sumatran rhinoceros today can be blamed fairly and squarely on those seeking their horns for various medical uses, and the other three species are not much better off.

Hunters have killed rhino for thousands of years in their quest for the valued horn, and the trade in this commodity can be traced back to the beginnings of civilization. Rhinoceros horn has been held in high esteem as a mystical artifact and curative drug for many thousands of years, even though medical science has repeatedly shown that the substance (which in reality is not horn at all but rather a tightly compacted compound of tubular hair-like filaments and keratin, similar in derivation to a cow's hoof), has none of the powers ascribed to it. In fact, taking a dose of rhino horn has the same medicinal value as chewing your fingernails.

The use of rhino horn is deeply seated in the cultures of many people in the Orient, and they will not be deprived of these traditional remedies without what they perceive to be good reason. Many Eastern people who today use Western drugs such as aspirin and antibiotics still firmly believe in the curative powers of powdered rhino horn. The horn's main use is not as an aphrodisiac as is the common belief, but rather as a treatment for colds and fever, headaches, arthritis and lumbago, particularly among the people of Japan, China and south-east Asia. Rhino horn is an important constituent of traditional Eastern medicines, still widely used today, and is commonly prescribed alongside or as an alternative to modern, scientifically based drugs.

(Dr Esmond Bradley Martin has conducted exhaustive research into the rhino horn trade on behalf of the World Wide Fund for Nature (WWF) and the International Union for the Conservation of Nature and Natural Resources (IUCN), and I am indebted to him for much of the information in these pages. He found that only in isolated areas of India was rhino horn used as an aphrodisiac, and then in such small quantities as to be inconsequential. Additionally, he could find no trace in Chinese traditional medicine texts of the use of rhino horn as an aphrodisiac, and became convinced that the belief held in the West that this is the major use of rhino horn is incorrect.)

The second most common use of rhino horn is in the making of traditional dagger handles in the Middle Eastern state of North Yemen (the Yemen Arab Republic). Virtually every Muslim man in Yemen carries this dagger, or *djambiyya*, which is not used so much in self-defence as in ceremonial dances and religious rituals. Rhino horn is held in the highest esteem as a material for making the handles; a wealthy Yemeni will pay as much as US$30 000 for a *djambiyya* with an ornately carved rhino horn handle, widely regarded as a status symbol among the newly rich.

Elsewhere in Asia there is widespread use of rhino products, including the skin, blood, dung and urine. Rhino hide is much sought after, with investigations into this trade showing that the majority of hide on sale is that of white rhino, originating in South Africa. Although some rhino have undoubtedly been poached for their skins it is not common practice, due mainly to the fact that the horns can be removed quickly after shooting the animal, but to skin a rhino can take considerable time. Medicinal use is made of rhino blood, dung and urine, particularly in India and Nepal, and zookeepers in these countries are known to collect the excrement of their captive rhino to sell to traditional healers.

STRINGENT MEASURES

This demand for and use of rhino products throughout the world's most heavily populated region, extending from Japan in the east through Korea, Taiwan, China, Hong Kong, Macao, the whole of south-east Asia, India, Nepal, Bhutan and North Yemen to Sudan in the west, poses an enormous threat to the world's few remaining rhino. In recent years all trade in rhino products from Africa has been declared illegal. Ironically, Namibia, currently striving so hard to save its few remaining desert black rhino, was perhaps the last country in Africa with a rhino population to outlaw the sale and export of rhino products; in 1983 the Namibian government sold almost 100 kilograms of rhino horn to a South African company at a price of US$460 per kilogram for export to Taiwan. On a larger scale, all trade in rhino products has been banned by the Convention on International Trade in Endangered Species of Wild Fauna and Flora (CITES), so that every country that is a signatory to this agreement which still imports or exports rhino products does so illegally.

THE 'RHINO WAR': EAST AND CENTRAL AFRICA

The illegality of trade in the horn has deterred neither the poachers nor the dealers and users, and Africa's rhino population has been slashed from more than 100 000 in 1960 to some 8 000 today, with the black rhino bearing the brunt of the poachers' onslaught. This increase in poaching has become serious only in the past 20-30 years, in the main as a result of a breakdown in law and order and an inability or disinterest in policing conservation regulations following independence from colonial rule throughout much of Africa.

The ease with which modern weapons, such as the AK-47 so popular with guerilla fighters, appear to be obtainable, combined with a lack of proper maintenance of the laws and an often dishonest government and judiciary has meant that poachers have operated with virtual impunity in many countries where rhino populations were once sizeable and stable. Until recently many African countries did not enforce the conservation laws on their statute books, and poachers and their masters and middlemen, when caught, more often than not tended to get off lightly. Gross corruption, and in some instances the involvement of senior government officials or their families, compounded the problem. Equally disturbing is the fact that in Kenya, for example, it is estimated that at least a third of all rhino poached in the country's reserves are killed by employees of the wildlife department. Similarly, several game guards of the Natal Parks Board have been convicted and jailed for poaching offences in recent years, while a former senior ranger in the Kruger National Park was charged in 1989 with poaching a number of rhino there.

However, even where the law and order situation is somewhat better, the appearance of highly organized and heavily armed commercial poaching gangs has led to the decimation of rhino populations, in particular that of the black rhino. Kenya, for example, had a population of some 20 000 black rhino as recently as 1969, protected in its popular and internationally famous national parks and reserves, with the Tsavo East and West national parks once boasting the world's largest single population of the species: as many as 9 000 animals. In the '70s, heavily armed gangs of poachers from Somalia invaded the parks and to this day are waging war against both the remaining rhino population and the out-gunned parks rangers and wardens. Kenya, along with Tanzania, Zambia and Zimbabwe, has been the main battle front in the 'rhino war', with Tsavo's rhino population now all but wiped out and the total population in the country estimated at few more than 200.

One bright spot in the Kenyan black rhino saga has been the success shown by the privately owned Solio Game Ranch where, well protected from poachers, black rhino numbers have increased from 25 in the '60s to as many as 100 today. Encouraged by the Solio example (and other private ranches), Kenyan wildlife authorities are now engaged in capturing black rhino in isolated areas and relocating them in well-guarded, fenced sanctuaries. In 1987 the government erected a high-voltage electrified fence around the small Lake Nakuru National Park and moved in 17 black rhino from other areas to join an existing pair. By 1990 matings had been observed among the new population and

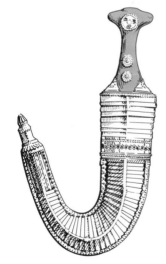

In North Yemen, a Middle Eastern state, nearly every man carries the traditional djambiyya, *a ceremonial symbol of manhood usually given by a father to his son at puberty. Rhino horn handles on these ceremonial daggers have long been symbols of wealth and status.*

63

a cow who was pregnant at the time of relocation had successfully given birth. A second, similar, sanctuary of 16 square kilometres has been set aside within Tsavo, and plans were afoot in 1989 to enclose part of the Aberdare National Park in the central highlands as a further black rhino sanctuary.

However, the security of such sanctuaries has to be regarded in the light of an occurrence which took place in the Meru National Park in Kenya in October 1988. A group of five white rhino relocated from the Umfolozi Game Reserve some years previously, which was herded into a stockade at night and had a 24-hour armed guard, was killed when a gang of 30 armed poachers attacked the homes of the warden and park rangers, opening fire with machine guns. As the park officials took cover, some of the gang members shot the five rhino and hacked off the horns with chainsaws before disappearing into the thick bush.

What can the survival chances of any rhino, anywhere, be in the face of such determination and firepower?

THE 'RHINO WAR': SOUTHERN AFRICA

With the rhino populations of East and Central Africa now diminished to almost negligible proportions, the 'rhino war' has moved south. Zimbabwe is currently waging a full-scale war against poachers in the Zambezi Valley, with a shoot-on-sight policy having been adopted by the government in its efforts to save both the elephant and the rhino populations. Zimbabwe's black rhino population was given as about 1 750 in 1989, but according to that country's wildlife department animals are being lost on an almost daily basis, and it was likely in early 1990 that the population was closer to 1 600.

Zimbabwe has now deployed armed soldiers to back up the wildlife department rangers, but this 'Operation Stronghold' has been severely hampered by a lack of financing. As Rowan Martin of Zimbabwe's Department of National Parks points out, it would cost as much as US$7 million a year to effectively patrol and protect the lower Zambezi Valley alone. Rhino conservation in Zimbabwe has reached the stage where it is primarily a case of attempting to save rhino by killing poachers, and relocating animals when logistically possible. In a style reminiscent of the Rhodesian bush war that led to the country's independence, well-equipped military-style armed 'sticks' of rangers are dropped by helicopter into poaching hotspots in rapid-deployment operations during which poachers are tracked to frequently fatal conclusions.

Swaziland, which has small, reintroduced populations of both black (six) and white (100) rhino, has already experienced a number of occurrences of poaching, although so far all the victims have been white rhino. By the end of 1989 at least eight incidents had been reported and the country's small but enthusiastic wildlife conservation department was gearing itself up for a heavier onslaught as populations further north in Africa become depleted and their protection increases. Hampered by a lack of both manpower and financial muscle, the Swazi authorities and noted local conservationist Ted Reilly have moved a number of rhino from the more open Hlane National Park to the better protection of other, smaller, reserves such as Mkhaya.

The desert black rhino of Namibia are unique in Africa and a concerted effort is under way to save them from the poachers' bullets. Figures released by that country's Directorate of Nature Conservation at the beginning of 1990 revealed that 32 black rhino had been poached in the Etosha National Park area during 1989 alone. Figures were not given for areas outside of the park, such as the Kaokoveld, where despite strict control poaching by local tribesmen and commercial hunters is known to be a problem. The rhino, elephant and giraffe of Kaokoland in Namibia are unique, for nowhere else on earth do they live in such arid, hostile conditions. It is remarkable that these animals, which usually prefer to drink once a day, have adapted to this harsh environment. It is for this reason that the desert rhino (and elephant) are considered a conservation priority, although it was not until the late '70s that poaching was noted as a serious problem in this region. Although in the early 1960s it was estimated only 100 rhino survived in Namibia (then South West Africa) these figures could not have been accurate for, using proper counting methods, it was recorded that more than 250 animals existed in the combined Kaokoland/Damaraland area in the mid-'70s.

However, by 1982 the poachers had taken their toll, and fewer than 60 black rhino remained in the region. The Endangered Wildlife Trust (EWT), founded by South African Clive Walker, now vice-chairman of the Rhino and Elephant Foundation, began an intensive campaign to publicize the plight of the desert rhino and elephant, and together with local conservationist Garth Owen-Smith initiated a major anti-poaching drive which continues today. Owen-Smith has been the prime mover in the concept of educating local tribespeople about the values of conservation, as well as in the introduction of an auxiliary game scout system. This system, funded by the EWT, has been effective in monitoring the movements of both the rhino and their hunters. The scouts are local tribespeople appointed by the headman of an area, and their duties include reporting on any vehicles moving through the region as well as game movements and suspicious happenings. These intensive monitoring and control policies have slowed the rate of attrition, and Namibia today stands alongside South Africa as one of the only two countries in Africa to have a successful black rhino conservation record.

The Damara Representative Council supports efforts at conservation and recognizes the tourism potential of the desert black rhino, particularly since the country's independence in 1990. Lately tribal headmen have been hiring their own auxiliary game guards to protect what they have come to regard as their own black rhino. (Although the animals occur on tribal lands, the game in reality belongs to the government.) Indications are that the new government of the previously South African-administered territory will attach high priority to tourism, and hence wildlife conservation, but it is too soon to be optimistic about the future of the desert black rhino.

Namibian authorities have attempted a number of novel and drastic anti-poaching methods, not the least of which has been the removal of the horns of living rhino. Despite expectations to the contrary, the animals adapted rapidly and appeared to suffer no ill effects. Rhino frequently break or lose their horns in the wild – the horn is not firmly attached to the bone of the skull as is the case with the true horns of antelope, for example, but grows from the skin – and the horn can grow again. The aesthetics of the operation are questionable, however: is it perhaps not better to see no rhino at all than to see one with its horns removed and its nose smeared with Stockholm tar? The philosophy of the Namibian conservationists is the exact reverse, in fact, for they believe it's better to see a rhino without horns than no rhino at all. At present, from a tourism point of view, these animals appear to have a curiosity value as visitors to the region apparently ask where they can see and photograph the de-horned rhino.

Says Blythe Loutit, founder of Namibia's Save the Rhino Trust Fund and recipient in 1989 of the David Scott Merit Award for her work with rhino in this region: 'To answer all the questions and criticisms [of the de-horning operation] one would need to be half rhino and half wizard.' Whatever the aesthetics, the de-horning exercise – Operation Bicornis – appears to have met with some success, for there have been fewer incidents of poaching since the start of the programme. Whether this can be put down to the actual de-horning, the publicity surrounding the operation, or the fact that on-the-ground surveillance in the region has also been stepped up considerably is anyone's guess . . . only the poachers themselves could tell.

As for the possible 'desocializing effect' on the rhino of horn removal, the one calf that has been born to a de-horned rhino in the area would have been conceived prior to the start of Operation Bicornis, so this remains to be seen. Black rhino courtship involves extensive ritual sparring, with the female giving as good as she gets. Whether a hornless cow might be hurt during courtship by a male with a horn has not been resolved, or even whether the male would still find her 'attractive'. Fortunately, the horn has little defensive use in the Kaokoveld for there are few predators (apart from man), and the rhino population is far from dense and there are thus unlikely to be many 'territorial' disputes.

Radio telemetry and aerial patrolling of the Kaokoveld as well as the Etosha area appear to be having a good effect, although the ramifications of Namibia's independence and the ending of the bush war, along with the subsequent availability of automatic weapons, remain to be seen. Namibian authorities have relocated several black rhino to undisclosed, less isolated, areas, 25 to the Waterberg Plateau Park, and 12 to two national parks, Vaalbos and Augrabies Falls, in the north-western Cape Province of South Africa, areas in which they last occurred some 150 years ago. The relocations have been a success, and new calves have been born to these populations.

65

Poachers, often poverty-stricken and starving but heavily armed with the automatic weapons so freely available after years of revolution and civil war in much of Africa, can earn as much as a year's wages from a pair of rhino horns. The only possible solution to the poaching problem seems to be in ending the demand rather than cutting off the supply.

BELOW: As part of their war against poaching, Namibian conservation authorities embarked in 1988 and 1989 on a controversial dehorning programme in Damaraland, home of the 'desert black rhino'. This experiment drew criticism, the reasons ranging from pure aesthetics to the possibility of interfering with the animals' social inter-relationships. Authorities there maintain however that the object is to save the rhino in the interim, and a dramatic decrease in the number of poaching incidents in the area to date indicates a large degree of success. Here a drugged rhino undergoes the horn removal . . . and the final result.

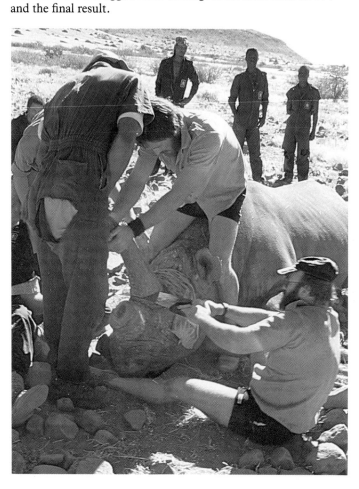

While all trade in rhino products has been banned by the CITES agreement, some countries have stockpiles of rhino horns garnered mainly from animals which died natural deaths. These countries face a dilemma in deciding how to dispose of the valuable commodity. Kenya, for example, has made expensive bonfires, burning piles of rhino horn and elephant ivory in anti-trade gestures which some find hard to understand.

Would a legal trading alternative, similar to the diamond industry's Central Selling Organization, not go some way to satisfying the undoubted demand, and earn much-needed revenue to improve policing and other conservation operations? The idea makes sense in terms of the 'sustainable yield' ethic of conservation policies.

67

By the beginning of 1990 South Africa had been spared the ravages of the 'rhino war'. South Africa and perhaps Namibia are the only countries in Africa to have shown a rhino population increase in recent years, but there are already signs that these countries will be the next major targets for international poaching rings. While most developing African countries have neither the money nor the resources to effectively protect their remaining rhino populations, South Africa does and already several high-profile projects and fund-raising campaigns are under way.

CONSERVATION TODAY: SOUTHERN POPULATIONS

The mere act of putting armed guards into the field, while perhaps acting as a deterrent to casual poachers, is not likely to stop the heavily armed and well-organized commercial operators. The morality – and effectiveness – of Zimbabwe's shoot-to-kill policy is also questionable: how right is it to kill people to save an animal, particularly when in most cases the poacher himself is merely a hired hand forced by economic necessity into serving the greed of his shadowy masters? Although it has been ascertained that the poacher himself gets perhaps only one per cent of what the horn eventually realizes in the markets of the East, even that is in many cases the equivalent of a year's wages for him . . . should the poacher be lucky enough to be able to obtain proper employment.

An out-and-out bush war cannot be regarded as a long-term or morally just strategy for the conservation of any game species, and agencies raising funds to save the rhino should ensure that their money is going to more positive areas such as captive breeding, research and monitoring projects, as well as the purchase of suitable ground for the reintroduction and relocation of rhino. It seems ludicrous, to me as well as to several others involved, that with hundreds of thousands of rands and dollars being committed to Save the Rhino funds, a black rhino monitoring programme to locate, identify and compile identikits of all black rhino in the Umfolozi-Hluhluwe-Corridor complex during 1989 had to be curtailed because there were insufficient funds available to keep a small helicopter aloft!

A conservation plan for the black rhino in South Africa and Namibia has been drawn up by the newly established Rhino Management Group (RMG), which comprises one representative from each of the southern African governmental conservation bodies: the National Parks Board, the Natal Parks Board, the Bophuthatswana Parks Board, the KwaZulu Bureau for Natural Resources, the Cape Chief Directorate of Nature and Environmental Conservation and the Namibian Department of Agriculture and Nature Conservation, all of which have black rhino in parks or reserves under their control. Sadly, political differences appear to be preventing Zimbabwe, with what is at present the largest black rhino population in Africa, from officially joining the group, although there are unofficial exchanges of information on an ongoing basis.

'The Conservation Plan For The Black Rhino, *Diceros bicornis*, in South Africa, the TBVC States and SWA/Namibia' was compiled for the RMG by Dr Martin Brooks of the Natal Parks Board, and lays down its aims as follows: a) to develop as rapidly as possible and conserve in the long term, a genetically viable population of at least 2 000 black rhino of the south-eastern ecotype, *Diceros bicornis minor*, in their natural habitat in the region; b) to develop as rapidly as possible, and conserve in the long term, a genetically viable population of at least 2 000 black rhino of the south-western ecotype, *D.b. bicornis*, in their natural habitat in the region; c) to develop as rapidly as possible and conserve a population of at least 100 of the north-eastern ecotype, *D.b. michaeli* in the wild in the region; d) to support captive breeding programmes for all three subspecies both within and outside southern Africa and the African continent, providing they can play a significant and sustained role in maintaining or improving the conservation status of the species.

The Natal Parks Board has already sent seven black rhino to a captive breeding project in Texas, USA and in June 1990 auctioned a breeding group of five black rhino to private landowners.

The RMG has established that there are an estimated 1 051 black rhino in the region – a third of the remaining world population – with about 650 in South Africa and the remainder in Namibia.

THE BOTTOM LINE

Today, however, understanding the trade in rhino horn and the uses thereof is perhaps the most important prerequisite of any campaign to save the (black) rhino, and I believe it is only by ending, or at the very least greatly curtailing, the demand for rhino horn and other rhino products, that the species will survive into the 21st century. As long as there is a demand for the product and there are rhino left on earth, somebody somewhere will be prepared to take the risks involved in killing them for profit. The threat of heavy jail sentences or even death in the field is not a big enough deterrent, a fact illustrated very clearly by an incident in January 1990 in Kathmandu, Nepal where there is a 20-year jail sentence for rhino poaching. With the rhino in that country's national parks extremely well protected, poachers turned to the Kathmandu Zoo, where two rhino, a cow and her calf, were poisoned and the horns stolen.

While Westerners may find it easy to dismiss Oriental beliefs in the curative powers of rhino horn (and other body parts), we should stop first to consider how many Westerners believe in the medicinal use of teas and brews made from leaves or fruits of exotic plants such as ginseng. Bear in mind too that the principal difference between Eastern and Western medical philosophies (from an Eastern point of view) is that Western science has synthesized and replaced with artificial drugs the active ingredients of their medicines, while Chinese and Japanese traditional doctors and their patients place their belief in natural, unadulterated ingredients with which they have had a long history of success. (Aspirin, for example, is a synthesized derivative of willow bark.) Additionally, even in Western medicine, faith in the treatment is an accepted function of healing, and it is the belief in the curative power of the rhino horn that is similarly important in Oriental medicine.

Compounding the problem in the East is the current swing away from Western medical practices as the harmful side-effects of popular drugs and the results of inadequate testing become evident. Now more than ever traditional Eastern societies are reverting to age-old beliefs. Today, formal training of medical practitioners in Japan and Korea covers both Western pharmacology and traditional practices, and it appears there will be a long uphill road to convincing the people of the Orient not to make use of illegal rhino products.

Perhaps one of the greatest chances for saving the rhino lies in convincing the traditional medical practitioners of the East to stop prescribing rhino horn as a drug, although so widespread is its use that these days preparations in both tablet and liquid form are freely available in most major cities in the Far East, such as Seoul, Hong Kong, Macao, Singapore, Bangkok, Tokyo, Osaka and Kuala Lumpur, as well as in the smaller centres. While Asian rhino horn is considered to be of higher quality, probably because the horns are much smaller in size than those of African rhino and hence considered to be more concentrated, the price difference has made African horn more popular in recent years. (Esmond Bradley Martin on a visit to Taiwan (the Republic of China) in 1988 found African rhino horn – from both black and white rhino – selling at US$4 660 a kilogram in Taipei, up from US$1 532 a kilogram in 1985, while the price of Asian rhino horn had climbed from US$23 927 to US$40 558 a kilogram during the same period.) He found too that medicine factories in mainland China, in cities such as Beijing, Tianjin and Guangzhou, have for many years been manufacturing patent medicines containing rhino horn. Exports of these and other traditional medicines earned China in excess of US$700 million in 1987 and are among the country's most important foreign exchange earners.

There is a strong belief that prices of horn will continue to rise steeply as Africa's rhino populations are depleted, with the consequence that traders are starting to stockpile the product as an investment for the future. The wholesale price of rhino horn in Taiwan is already double that paid by importers elsewhere, and the middlemen in the illegal trade in Africa have stepped up the financial incentives to poachers in their efforts to meet the demand.

One well-known and popular medication, manufactured in Johore, Malaysia, is the 'Three Legs Brand Rhinoceros Horn Anti-Fever Water' which advises on its label that 'This medicine is carefully prepared from the best selected Rhinoceros Horn and Anti-Fever Drugs, and under the direct supervision of Experts. This wonderful medicine acts like a charm in giving immediate relief to those suffering from: Malaria, High Temperature, Fever affecting the Heart and Four Limbs, Against Climate Giddiness, Insanity, Toothache, etc'. With such proclaimed powers, there is little wonder at its popularity!

Efforts have been made by various foreign agencies, including the IUCN, WWF and United States Agency for International Development, to find substitutes for rhino horn and persuade the various users to accept these. So far limited success has been achieved in substituting the horns of saiga antelope (*Saiga tatarica*) and water buffalo (*Bubalus arnee*); in the latter part of the '80s there was a slight fall in rhino horn retail prices in most of south-east Asia, primarily, it was hoped, because of a fall in demand linked to a growing acceptance of the much cheaper substitutes, and not because of a greater availability of rhino horns. (Taiwan was the only country to show consistent increases in price; significantly, that country is today regarded as the world's major buyer of illegal rhino horn, even though it banned all imports and exports of rhino products in August 1985.)

Huge increases in the penalties for dealing in rhino horn were introduced throughout South Africa and Namibia in 1989, with heavy jail sentences and fines of up to R100 000 now the norm. It remains to be seen, however, if international diplomatic pressure and the efforts of organizations such as WWF, IUCN and CITES will have any serious effect on the trade in the East, for although nearly every country has banned the import and export of rhino products, little is done to enforce these laws. And while the domestic sale of rhino products within Eastern countries continues − under the pretence of 'using up existing stocks' − there appears to be little hope of stopping the slaughter.

Until recent years North Yemen was considered to be the world's major consumer of African rhino products, primarily the horns of black rhino. Formerly an extremely poor Middle Eastern state, a republic was declared in 1962 after the centuries-old religious aristocracy was overthrown. Following an eight-year civil war which ended in 1970, many Yemenis began working as migrant labourers in the neighbouring Saudi Arabian oilfields, with the inflow of foreign earnings peaking at approximately US$3 million a day in 1978. The discovery of oil within the country further increased the spending power of the people. A Muslim Arab state, nearly every man carries the traditional *djambiyya*, a ceremonial symbol of manhood usually given by a father to his son at puberty.

Rhino horn handles on these ceremonial daggers have long been symbols of wealth and status, and prior to the revolution could be afforded only by the rich and powerful. However, with the sudden wealth of the country, Yemeni men could afford these status-elevating dagger handles and it was primarily because of this sudden increase in demand that rhino poaching escalated so sharply in the 1970s, along with a rise in the wholesale price of the horn from US$35 in 1969 to more than US$1 500 a kilogram in 1989. According to official records, North Yemen imported more than 22 tons of rhino horn between 1970 and 1977, the product of the death of perhaps 8 000 rhino. Ironically, few Yemenis have probably seen even a picture of a rhino or have any concept of its appearance, and the commonly used term for rhino horn, *zurraf*, is in fact the Arabic word for giraffe.

However, unlike the situation in the Far East, the problem in North Yemen appears to be countering a practical argument rather than a traditional or superstitious belief: after centuries of experience the Yemenis have found that there is nothing as good as rhino horn for durability as well as appearance. Hilts made of rhino horn are more resistant to wear and tear than any other natural substance, and the older they get the better they look, taking on a translucency similar to amber with age. So long as Yemeni men believe rhino horn is the best material for their *djambiyya* hilts conservationists will have difficulty persuading them not to use it.

Although not a CITES signatory at the time, the North Yemen government banned the import of rhino horn as far back as August 1982, but little was done to enforce this law and it merely served to push the price up by increasing the bribes needed to pay customs officials at the port of entry. Dealers and *djambiyya* manufacturers continued to flaunt the law openly, and until the government banned the export of rhino products in 1987, the dagger makers even recouped some of their outlay on horn by selling offcuts and shavings to dealers in the Far East. Further action taken by the government of North Yemen in 1986 included the implementation of a six-point strategy aimed at gradually eliminating the rhino horn trade. The WWF and United States Agency for International Development (USAID) launched a joint project in Yemen in 1987 to examine the uses of rhino horn and find a suitable alternative.

The curse of the consumer world, inflation, appears to have helped the rhino in certain respects and with rising prices in North Yemen and a decline in the value of the Yemen currency against the US dollar, it now appears fewer and fewer people can afford rhino horn, for unlike its use as a medication, where only a gram or two is prescribed at a time, the cheapest rhino horn hilt starts at US$1 500. A handle carved from the horn of water buffalo, on the other hand, costs only about US$10.

Dr Esmond Bradley Martin has spent time in North Yemen attempting to persuade dagger craftsmen to utilize other materials for the hilts. He has also requested the religious leader of the republic, the Grand Mufti, to issue a decree stating it is against the will of God to totally eliminate any living species, which will be the ultimate end if the illegal use of rhino horn continues. However, as with the traders in the Far East, the increasing rarity of rhino horn has led to many people in North Yemen realizing its investment value, and the feeling now is that if rhino become extinct their daggers will become priceless!

Conservation agencies do report a slight decrease in the demand for rhino horn in the Arab state though, as the country becomes increasingly Westernized and the carrying of the *djambiyya* in everyday Western attire is no longer so important. With some 50 000 Yemeni boys coming of age every year, and thus 'earning' their own *djambiyya*, we can only hope Western fashions remain in vogue.

TO SELL OR NOT TO SELL

It is the trade in rhino products that has led to the demise of Africa's black rhino populations and it would appear that no matter how illegal, it continues. Elephant are no better off and these animals are being slaughtered almost as fast as rhino, a state of affairs that led to a worldwide ban on ivory trading being introduced by CITES in 1989.

But does CITES work? By all appearances, in stopping the trade in rhino horn and thus saving the endangered (black) rhino, it has failed. Despite international treaties the trade continues, either because importing countries turn a blind eye or leave loopholes in their laws, or as a result of downright corruption from junior civil servant level right up to senior government officials.

Countries with good records in conserving their wildlife and preventing poaching are being lumped together with those that have proved ineffective and weak – in other words, there is one law for all. However, this is not always fair to all. Consider the new ivory trade ban: countries in East and Central Africa, where elephant are being killed at alarming rates and poaching is described as having reached crisis proportions, obviously have not managed to police their reserves, educate their people or conserve their wildlife as successfully as countries like Botswana, Zimbabwe, Namibia and South Africa. In these southern African countries elephant continue to increase in numbers and culling is considered to be an essential aspect of their management. South Africa and Zimbabwe, two of the worst hit by the ban on ivory trading, argue that the income from the ivory they sell after culling operations is ploughed back into conservation: why should they suffer, they ask, because Kenya or Tanzania, for example, have not done a good job of protecting their herds? (Botswana, which for several years has not allowed elephant hunting and has had no culling operations, now appears to have an elephant population in excess of 50 000, which is causing great habitat destruction, and hunting and culling operations are expected to begin soon.)

The sustained utilization of natural resources is an internationally recognized precept of conservation; in other words, wildlife must pay its own way. The countries that have managed their elephant populations well are now being lumped with those that have not . . . to the detriment of the former.

In July 1989 Kenyan President Daniel Arap Moi torched more than 18 tons of ivory (worth more than US$10 million) that country's wildlife authorities had in stock, either confiscated from poachers or retrieved from dead elephants; in January 1990 he set fire to a stack of rhino horn worth almost US$6 million. The president said this was done

There is a strong belief that prices of horn will continue to rise steeply as Africa's rhino populations are depleted, with the consequence that traders are starting to stockpile the product as an investment for the future. The wholesale price of rhino horn in Taiwan is already double that paid by importers elsewhere, and the middlemen in the illegal trade in Africa have increased the financial incentives to poachers in their efforts to meet the demand.

71

to discourage poaching, so that 'we can pass on our heritage to our children'. Fine words, indeed, but was the gesture sensible?

The Natal Parks Board, according to many reports, currently has a stockpile of rhino horn worth close on US$10 million. Almost all these horns were recovered from rhino that had died natural deaths in the wild, and in line with the sustainable yield ethic – that wildlife must pay its way – would inject a considerable boost into the conservation coffers. Does Dr George Hughes, Chief Director of the Natal Parks Board, sell or burn? Do the Namibian conservation authorities, strapped for cash to finance their efforts, market the horns they remove from the desert black rhino and so gain the capital to continue their struggle against poaching? Could the Kenyan wildlife authorities not have made good use of the US$16 million that went up in smoke?

These countries are, in more ways than one, on the horns of a dilemma. It is not debatable that the trade in rhino horn has been the cause of the rapid decline in rhino populations in Africa. Simply, it seems that if we get rid of the trade we end the poaching. Is it morally defensible to decry the sale of rhino products on the one hand and sell them on the other?

I believe it is. Just as the illegal trade by unlicenced persons in unwrought gold or uncut diamonds is countered by the legal, controlled trade by licenced dealers, so I believe rhino horn should be marketed. Perhaps the best way to approach the illegal trade in rhino horn would be to institute a legal alternative. An international 'Central Selling Organization' body, set up to control the marketing of both rhino horn and ivory, could at the same time undercut the profits of the black marketeers and earn considerable income for the cause of conservation. While there are elephant and rhino there will be poachers prepared to hunt them, but I am positive that a strictly controlled legal trade will diminish the numbers of poachers, particularly in combination with heavy penalties for poaching and, in particular, for illegal trading.

The white rhino, largest of the five rhino species and today also the most numerous after being close to extinction at the turn of this century.

The future

Can Africa do for the black rhino what the Natal Parks Board has done for the white? This appears to be the major question in conservation circles today – and the answer is an optimistic yes. Considering that the white rhino population was down to as few as 50 earlier this century, and these located in only one small area, the prognosis for the black rhino should be hopeful, if not yet bright.

Kenya's wildlife authority, now augmented by the country's military and headed by the livewire Dr Richard Leakey, appears to have secured the future of at least a fraction of its black rhino population, albeit in heavily guarded and often electrified stockades. This awareness and these good intentions are backed by international funding, and while the sight of the typically heavy-horned East African black rhino roaming the plains will probably not be common for many years yet, it appears likely that some time in the future tourists will be able to thrill to the experience once more. The East African Wildlife Society, referring to the poaching of rhino and elephant – both valuable tourist attractions – in Kenya told a news conference in 1988, 'Poaching is not merely a pity or something to be regretted; it is economic sabotage with far-reaching and lasting effects on the prosperity, stability and success of our country. It is a national crisis.' These are words that should be heeded by the governments of all countries in Africa, for wildlife is our heritage.

The prognosis for Tanzania and Zambia is bleak, for these countries have already lost most of their black rhino and do not have the co-ordinated anti-poaching methods of Kenya or the countries of southern Africa. The sight of a black rhino roaming the plains of the Selous National Park and Serengeti or Kenya's Amboseli National Park with the snow-capped peak of Kilimanjaro in the background, is one of the indelible images of Africa, but it is one that, barring a miracle, is likely to become little more than a photographic record of what once was.

In Zimbabwe, the bush war that led to independence has become a war to save the rhino. In the Zambezi Valley poachers are shot on sight in a desperate attempt to stop the slaughter of that country's remaining black rhino, but still the numbers fall daily. Where possible, black rhino are being captured for relocation to better protected areas further from the Zambian border, from where it is claimed the majority of poachers originate. Zimbabwe currently has Africa's largest black rhino population and should be able to save at least some of it. It is a great pity that, in the words of the Rhino Management Group, 'political differences may prevent an interchange of animals across the Limpopo' for this could be one of the solutions to the problems faced by Zimbabwe's wildlife managers.

The political uncertainty in Namibia immediately following the country's independence does not bode well for its black rhino population, despite the dedication of a small band of conservationists, both government and non-government. The importance of the activities of Rudi and Blythe Loutit, Garth Owen-Smith and several others in instilling in the rural tribespeople an awareness of the future value of wildlife as a source of tourist revenue cannot be overstressed. International influence through organizations such as the WWF, IUCN and CITES should also assist in securing the future of the desert rhino, along with the equally unique desert elephant and giraffe, and perhaps the balance can be tipped slightly in their favour. Namibia's rhino population, although at present regarded as stable, will require careful monitoring in the years ahead.

South Africa has, undoubtedly, the best conservation record in Africa, and the simple fact that this country's annual expenditure on conservation is some US$85 million, compared with US$75-million for the rest of Africa, illustrates the point. But South Africa has little room for complacency: despite thus far being little affected by the ravages further north in Africa, there have already been isolated incidents of rhino poaching in several areas as well as a number of arrests for trafficking in both horn and ivory. In fact, according to Dr Esmond Bradley Martin, South Africa may have taken over from Burundi as the major entry point to the international black market in rhino horn, particularly considering this country's close trading links with Taiwan. Traders in Taiwan told Martin quite openly that horn was imported on direct flights from Johannesburg, to where it is allegedly channelled from Zambia, Angola, Zaïre and East Africa, via the Kazungula border post into Botswana and onwards to the Transvaal. According to South African authorities little can be done to stop this through-trade, for in most cases the contraband is hidden in sealed containers which they are unable to open because of international freight-handling agreements.

All of South Africa's black rhino are kept in fenced and patrolled game reserves and national parks, and current monitoring programmes aimed at compiling comprehensive identikits of every animal will go a long way to keeping a close eye on the situation. In 1989 I participated in such a programme in the Umfolozi-Hluhluwe-Corridor complex, and in barely a week we managed to locate and categorize more than 140 black rhino. The programme is to be extended in 1990, with the probability that unidentifiable animals will be darted and notches cut in their ears. The identikits will assist wildlife managers in monitoring the movements of each animal, as well as births and deaths, and indicate when the animal is no longer there.

None of South Africa's populations, however, can be considered totally safe, and biologists consider only populations of 500 or more to be genetically ideal. At present the largest single population in the country is that of the Umfolozi-Hluhluwe-Corridor complex, with an estimated 220-250 black rhino. The complex has an estimated total carrying capacity of some 300, but it is agreed that black rhino breed at their maximum rate when populations are kept at 50-60 per cent of optimum capacity. It is for this reason that black rhino are regularly captured in the Natal reserves for relocation.

Only the Kruger National Park at present has the ability to sustain a really large black rhino population, and the present population of 160-odd has a long way to go to reach its projected carrying capacity of 3 500. According to a paper by Dr Hall-Martin this population is breeding exceptionally well and will soon be the largest single population in South Africa. The Kruger National Park black rhino have grown from an initial gift of 20 from the Natal Parks Board in 1971, followed by 12 from Zimbabwe in 1972. A further 50 donated by the Natal Parks Board over subsequent years, and 10 from KwaZulu's Ndumu Game Reserve in 1989, has strengthened this original nucleus.

The South African National Parks Board is, incidentally, the only conservation authority in the world with populations under its control of three of the four recognized black rhino subspecies, with only *D. b. longipes* (which could now be extinct) not represented.

The manipulation of black rhino populations to sustain maximum reproduction is of great importance for the future of the species, and should play a major role in the Rhino Management Group's intentions of building up populations of 2 000 of both *D. b. minor* and *D. b. bicornis* in southern Africa. In the wild, black rhino appear to breed at rates of between three and 10 per cent a year: this is significant when one realizes that it would take almost 40 years to raise the present population of about 600 *D. b. minor* in South Africa to the desired 2 000 if the rate remains at three per cent, whereas at eight per cent it will take a mere 12-14 years.

However, all this will be of little avail if attention is not paid to the equally important aspect of educating and obtaining the support and co-operation of rural communities . . . and here educating does not mean teaching rural Africans the white man's values. Many impoverished rural Africans regard game reserves and conservation areas as part of their problem, barring access to grazing, raw materials and game products, particularly in view of the punitive policing of these areas. Perhaps if some of the money going into building up the force of game rangers and increasing policing were to be redirected at integrating local communities into conservation programmes and providing direct benefits, some headway towards breaking the impasse could be made. Certainly, reinforcing game guards, buying guns and erecting electrified fences can only be a short-term holding option. Making the wildlife directly valuable to people surrounding the reserves, so that they themselves will want to cultivate it and protect it for reasons that make practical sense to them, is the only long-term answer to the problem. The success of Garth Owen-Smith and the Loutits in Namibia in this regard stands like a beacon for all to see.

Behind the scenes

'Save the Rhino' has become the clarion call of conservationists worldwide, and a plethora of fund-raising and other bodies has leapt to the cause. South Africa, Namibia, Zimbabwe, Kenya, Zambia and Tanzania all have various organizations involved in rhino conservation efforts.

WORLD WIDE FUND FOR NATURE (WWF)

Formerly the World Wildlife Fund, the WWF has 24 affiliate organizations in countries throughout the world and can be regarded as the major force in efforts to protect all forms of nature. Through its offices – and a network of contacts in some of the highest government offices in the world – this organization has co-ordinated many of the most notable conservation efforts in recent years. Its weight behind campaigns to save the black rhino as well as all four other rhino species can be regarded as being of the utmost importance. The WWF is currently involved in rhino conservation efforts in Nepal, India, Java, Sabah, Zimbabwe, East Africa, Zaïre and Zambia.

INTERNATIONAL UNION FOR THE CONSERVATION OF NATURE AND NATURAL RESOURCES (IUCN) (now known as THE WORLD CONSERVATION UNION)

The IUCN, based in Geneva, Switzerland, is, like the WWF, an international body. However, where the WWF is primarily a fund-raising and public awareness organization, the IUCN functions mainly as a scientific and research co-ordinator, and bodies such as the African Elephant and Rhino Specialist Group fall under its auspices. The IUCN is also actively involved in attempts to find substitutes for rhino horn in the constitution of traditional medicines as well as in the dagger handles used by men in North Yemen.

CONVENTION ON INTERNATIONAL TRADE IN ENDANGERED SPECIES OF WILD FAUNA AND FLORA (CITES)

CITES is an international convention banning trade in all species listed by the IUCN as endangered. Countries are asked to voluntarily become signatories of CITES, whereafter any trade by that country in products listed under the convention becomes illegal. Other than to offer a high profile to CITES-listed wildlife products, the convention has not been a major success, mainly because of difficulties in enforcing its laws.

CITES Appendix I species are those that are threatened with immediate extinction; CITES Appendix II designates species not currently threatened with extinction but which could become so unless the trade is strictly regulated.

SOUTHERN AFRICAN NATURE FOUNDATION (SANF)

The SANF is effectively the South African arm of the WWF and acts primarily to raise funds and finance worthwhile conservation projects, and to co-ordinate WWF activities within southern Africa. Its 'Save the Desert Dwellers' campaign is specifically aimed at funding the survival of Namibia's unique desert rhino and elephant.

NAMIBIAN NATURE FOUNDATION

This is the sister organization of the SANF and functions in much the same manner within Namibia.

ENDANGERED WILDLIFE TRUST (EWT)

The EWT is a private fund-raising body, based in Johannesburg, which raises money to fund urgent research and conservation activities involving endangered species throughout southern Africa. Founded almost 16 years ago, it is currently heavily involved in efforts to save the black rhino of southern Africa. In particular, it is giving extensive support to the Namibian Wildlife Trust's rhino project, especially in funding the auxiliary game scout system. The EWT has been actively engaged in black rhino support for many years, and is one of the pioneer non-governmental bodies in this regard.

RHINO AND ELEPHANT FOUNDATION (REF)

The REF is a high-profile fund-raising body, based in Johannesburg, that has specifically targeted rhino and elephant for protection. It is currently engaged in a two-year Project Rhino campaign in which it is endeavouring both to raise a substantial amount of money for rhino conservation as well as to create greater awareness of the plight of the black rhino. The REF is involved in funding operations in South Africa, Zimbabwe, Mozambique and Namibia.

EAST AFRICAN WILDLIFE SOCIETY (EAWLS)

The EAWLS is based in Nairobi, Kenya, and has done much in recent years to attempt to awaken East African governments to the threat of poaching to both elephant and black rhino. It raises substantial amounts of money through various fund-raising efforts and operates a Save the Rhino Fund for specific donations to black rhino conservation efforts.

WILDLIFE SOCIETY OF SOUTHERN AFRICA

The Wildlife Society of SA has launched a Save the Rhino Trust Fund. It was involved in a highly successful programme of inviting schools and businesses to 'sponsor' an individual rhino, thereby raising much needed money for, primarily, Namibian efforts to conserve the desert rhino.

RHINO RESCUE TRUST

The trust runs offices in both England and Kenya, raising funds for rhino projects in East Africa.

ZOO CHECK CHARITABLE TRUST

Zoo Check, based in Surrey, England, is another fund-raising body that raises money for wildlife conservation, including save-the-rhino efforts worldwide.

THE DAVID SHELDRICK WILDLIFE APPEAL

Based in Nairobi, Kenya, the David Sheldrick Appeal has been associated with numerous conservation projects in Kenya in past years, and has now thrown considerable effort into helping with rhino and elephant conservation. The Sheldrick family, who once raised an orphaned black rhino, have a special affinity for these animals.

Scientific data

White rhino

Scientific name: *Ceratotherium simum*
Subspecies: *C.s. simum* (southern Africa)
   C.s. cottoni (Zaïre, Sudan?)
Other common names: Square-lipped rhino, Grass rhino, *Witrenoster* (Afrikaans), *Mkhombe* (Zulu), *Tshukudu* (Tswana and Sotho), *Faro* (Swahili)

DIMENSIONS

Length: 3,6-4,2 metres
Height at shoulder: 1,5-1,85 metres
Weight: 2 100-3 000 kilograms (bull),
   1 400-1 700 (cow)
Horn length (average-maximum):
   95-200 cm

IDENTIFICATION

Large and bulky, the white rhino has a broad, square muzzle and an elongated head which it carries low. There is a large pronounced hump on the back of the neck. Two horns, one behind the other, are mounted on the face; the front horn is much longer than the rear one, and sometimes projects forward. The legs are shorter than those of the black rhino. The ears are pointed and trumpet-like, and fringed with hair. Dull 'battleship' grey in colour, the animal often takes on the hue of its last mudbath.

HABITAT

Open grasslands, particularly short-grassed areas, with bushy areas for shade and cover. The white rhino needs a good water supply, and will walk considerable distances to drink.

HABITS

Bulls are territorial and solitary; cows are comparatively sociable and frequently found in groups of three to 10, and occasionally up to 18. Territorial bulls occupy clearly defined territories which they defend fiercely against intruding dominant bulls; subordinate bulls are tolerated as long as they remain submissive. White rhino make use of communal dung heaps (middens) and these have territorial significance when used by the territorial bulls. They drink at night but feed intermittently throughout the day, alternating with periods of rest. Like the black rhino, they enjoy wallowing; unlike their black cousins, who prefer to take the sun, white rhino prefer lying up in the shade.

FOOD

White rhino are grazers and prefer short grasses. They drink daily when water is available, and will travel long distances to and from waterholes, usually keeping to the same path.

VOICE

White rhinoceros communicate by means of 10 discernibly different sounds, six vocal and four aspiratory. These can be described as snorts, snarls, pants, hics, squeals, shrieks, squeaks, whines, gruff squeals and a 'gasp-puff'.

REPRODUCTION

The gestation period is about 16 months. A single calf, weighing about 45 kg, may be born at any time of the year. There is no distinct breeding season. The calf suckles for over a yar, and remains with the mother until the birth of the next calf. Young calves run ahead of their mothers when on the move.

DISTRIBUTION

The northern white rhino (*C.s. cottoni*) is restricted today to 26 animals in Garamba National Park, Zaïre, and four in southern Sudan, although formerly widespread in Zaïre, Sudan, Chad and Uganda. Reduced from its original range throughout South Africa, Angola, Botswana, Zimbabwe, Mozambique and Namibia to a handful of survivors in the Umfolozi Game Reserve in Natal, South Africa at the turn of the century, the southern white rhino (*C.s. simum*) today boasts a population of more than 4 600 and is one of the great conservation success stories. It has been reintroduced to game reserves and farms in most of its former range in southern Africa. The Umfolozi-Hluhluwe-Corridor complex today contains the largest population of white rhino in the world (nearing 2 000).

STATUS

The northern white rhino is in immediate danger of extinction and has been classified by CITES as an Appendix I species. The southern white rhino has been classified by CITES as Appendix II (not currently threatened with extinction but could become so unless trade is strictly regulated).

Black rhino

Scientific name: *Diceros bicornis*
Subspecies: *D.b. minor* (southern Africa)
  D.b. bicornis (Namibia, northern Cape)
  D.b. michaeli (East Africa, Addo
    Elephant National Park)
  D.b. longipes (Central Africa)
Other common names: Hook-lipped
rhino, Prehensile-lipped rhino, *Swart-renoster* (Afrikaans), *Bhejane* (Zulu),
Tshukudu (Tswana), *Ngava* (Herero) and
Faro (Swahili).

DIMENSIONS

Length: 3,0-3,8 metres
Height at shoulder: 1,4-1,8 metres
Weight: 995-1 360 kilograms
Horn length (average-maximum):
  50-135 cm

IDENTIFICATION

The black rhino's head is shorter and is
held higher than that of the white rhino;
its ears are more rounded and smaller
than those of its cousin; and it is less
bulky and lacks the pronounced hump on
back of the neck. The distinctive hooked
top lip and pointed muzzle aid in identi-
fication. It can be further distinguished
from the white species by its erect, hollow-
backed stance and longer legs. Two horns
are mounted on the face, one behind the
other, the rear horn frequently being as
long as the anterior one. In some areas
(in Zululand and Kenya) specimens may
have raw, bloody lesions on the chest and
sides. In colour the black rhino is dull
grey-brown.

HABITAT

Black rhino prefer shrubby, open areas
with dense thickets for shelter and ready
availability of water. They will drink
daily, although in some areas such as the
Kaokoveld in Namibia can go three to
four days without drinking, obtaining
much of their moisture needs from
succulent plants.

HABITS

Black rhino occur either singly or in
family groups comprising a mother and
calf, and occasionally also an older calf.
Most active at night and in the early
mornings and late afternoons, in the summer months they spend a large part of the
day lying in mud wallows; in winter they
lie in the sun seeking shade only in the
hottest part of the day. They are not territorial, but use communal dung heaps
(middens), probably as a social indication
to other rhino of their presence in the
area. Bulls frequently scatter their dung
with vigorous rearward kicks of their
hind legs, leaving deep scrapes in the
soil. Bad-tempered and fractious, they
need little provocation to charge.

FOOD

Black rhino are browsers, using the prehensile, hooked upper lip to grasp leaves
and branches and manipulate them into
the mouth. They appear to be particularly fond of certain scrub acacia varieties
and, in Zululand, of the poisonous tamboti (*Spirostachys africana*). They will also
eat fruits and bulbs, and occasionally
grass, particularly fresh shoots after the
spring rains. Their food requirements
dictate habitat suitability: where the vegetation grows too high for them to browse
effectively, black rhino will move away
or die off.

VOICE

A variety of grunts, squeals, snorts,
snarls and puffs, mostly in association
with courtship or disputes. Also a high-
pitched mewing uttered by calves, usually
when in distress.

REPRODUCTION

The gestation period is about 15 months,
with no fixed breeding season. A single
calf, weighing about 25-40 kg, is born. It
remains with its mother until the next
calf is due, usually for about three to five
years. Calves suckle until well over a year
old. The calf follows the mother when
on the move.

DISTRIBUTION

Formerly widespread throughout Africa,
even to the slopes of Table Mountain,
today the black rhino is seriously threatened except where protected in game
reserves in South Africa. The population
has dropped from as many as 100 000 in
1960 to fewer than 3 500 in 1990, in the
whole of Africa. Today only Zimbabwe,
Namibia, South Africa and Kenya have
populations of any note.

STATUS

Seriously endangered, the black rhino has
been classified by CITES in Appendix I
(threatened with extinction). Only in
South Africa and Namibia, where conservation authorities have joined forces to
form the Rhino Management Group, does
the prognosis for the black rhino hold
hope. Zimbabwe, with the largest black
rhino population of any country (1 600),
is experiencing severe poaching losses
on an almost daily basis and prospects for
their salvation are bleak. Latest figures
estimate populations at 1 600 in Zimbabwe, 650 in South Africa, 450 in
Namibia, 200 in Kenya, 40 in Zambia,
and possibly 200 in Mozambique.

Indian rhino

Scientific name: *Rhinoceros unicornis*
Other common name: Great one-horned rhino

DIMENSIONS

Length: 2,1-4,2 metres
Height at shoulder: 1,1-2,0 metres
Weight: 1 500-2 000 kilograms
Horn length (average-maximum):
20-61 cm

IDENTIFICATION

This massive, thick-skinned species has heavy folds in the skin at the neck which give the impression of its being armour-plated. The hide is covered with knobby tubercules. The Indian rhino has only one horn, which is short and blunt, but it also has long, pointed incisor teeth (absent in the African rhino) which it may bare in threat displays. It is grey in colour.

HABITAT

Thickets and forests in association with marshlands; cane and reed thickets. It is never found far from water.

HABITS

The Indian rhino is solitary and unsociable, apart from mother and calf unions. It is both a browser and a grazer, with grass making up 80 per cent of its diet. It loves water and swims readily, as well as wallowing in mud. Although not territorial, it does utilize communal dung heaps (middens), probably to advise others of its presence.

FOOD

Browse and graze: grass, cane shoots, leaves, twigs, fruit, water hyacinth and agricultural crops where available.

VOICE

Snarls, growls and squeals, usually associated with courtship or fighting.

REPRODUCTION

There is no distinct breeding season. Courtship is marked by ritualized violence. The gestation period is about 16 months, after which a single calf, weighing approximately 40 kg, is born. Twins have been recorded, but these are extremely rare.

DISTRIBUTION

Formerly widely distributed throughout southern Asia, the Indian rhino is now found only in national parks in India and Nepal.

STATUS

With a world population of 2 000, the Indian rhino is considered a seriously endangered species, with a CITES Appendix I classification.

Javan rhino

Scientific name: *Rhinoceros sondaicus*
Other common name: Lesser one-horned Asian rhino

DIMENSIONS

Length: 3,5 metres
Height at shoulder: 1,8 metres
Weight: 1 300 kilograms
Horn length (average-maximum):
25-27 cm

IDENTIFICATION

Smaller but similar in appearance to the Indian rhino, the Javan rhino has heavy folds in its skin but lacks the knobby tubercules of the Indian rhino. The single horn, mounted on the face, is very short and stubby and is present only in males, females possessing little more than a small raised knob. The Javan rhino can be distinguished by its almost scaly, segmented appearance and its prehensile upper lip.

HABITAT

Tropical forests.

HABITS

Believed to be territorial, Javan rhino do not utilize middens but mark their territory by urine-spraying. They enjoy wallowing in mudbaths and are never found far from water. This species has never been successfully studied in the wild, despite numerous attempts.

FOOD

The Javan rhino is a browser and uses its prehensile top lip for grasping leaves, twigs and cane shoots.

VOICE

Unknown.

REPRODUCTION

Unknown, but likely to be similar to the Indian rhino.

DISTRIBUTION

Formerly common and widespread from India throughout south-east Asia, the Javan rhino was hunted to the brink of extinction and today survives only in the Ujung Kulon National Park in Java, and possibly in Vietnam.

STATUS

With a total world population of only 50 animals, the Javan rhino has been classified by CITES as an Appendix I species.

Sumatran rhino

Scientific name: *Dicerorhinus sumatrensis*
Other common name: Asian two-horned
rhino

DIMENSIONS

Length: 2,5-2,8 metres
Height at shoulder: 1,0-1,5 metres
Weight: 800 kilograms
Horn length (average-maximum):
    25-80 cm

IDENTIFICATION

The smallest of all the rhino, the Sumatran species is covered with dense, dark,
reddish-brown hair. It has two horns
mounted on its face, one behind the other.
The horns are short, blunt and rounded.
It has a prehensile upper lip.

HABITAT

Tropical forests.

HABITS

Very little is known about this species as
it has never been successfully studied in
the wild. It is secretive and unsociable,
apart from mother and calf unions. It
wallows frequently and is never found far
from water. It will 'walk down' small
trees to reach new shoots at the crown.

FOOD

The Sumatran rhino is a browser, feeding
on leaves, twigs, fruit and cane shoots.

VOICE

Unknown.

REPRODUCTION

Unknown; the first scientific studies of
the species are now under way in the Tabin
Reserve in Sabah, where captive animals
are being monitored. It is unlikely that
the gestation period differs much from the
15-16 months of the other rhino species, or
that more than one calf is born at a time.

DISTRIBUTION

Formerly widespread throughout Sumatra, Borneo, Malaya, Burma, Thailand,
Laos, Cambodia, Bengal and Assam,
today the species is sparsely scattered in
reserves in Indonesia, Malaysia and
Burma, and Thailand.

STATUS

With a total world population of between
400 and 900, the Sumatran rhino is seriously endangered and classified by CITES
in Appendix I. There are hopes of reintro-
ducing captive-bred animals into the wild.

Bibliography

ANDERSSON, CHARLES JOHN (1856). *Lake Ngami.* Hurst & Blackett, London.

ASTLEY MABERLY, CHARLES T. (1963). *The Game Animals of Southern Africa.* T. Nelson & Sons Ltd, London.

BEARD, PETER (1963). *The End of the Game.* Collins, London.

BROOKS, DR P M. (1989). Conservation Plan for the Black Rhinoceros *Diceros bicornis* in South Africa, the TBVC states and SWA/Namibia. (A policy statement and working document for conservation agencies managing black rhinoceros populations.) Rhino Management Group, Pretoria.

BURTON, RICHARD F. (1860). *The Lake Regions of Central Africa; A Picture of Exploration* (2 vols). Longman, London.

CAPSTICK, PETER HATHAWAY (1978). *Death in the Long Grass.* Methuen Paperbacks Ltd, London.

CORNWALLIS HARRIS, CAPTAIN WILLIAM (1840; reprinted 1969). *Portraits of the Game and Wild Animals of Southern Africa.* A. A. Balkema, Cape Town.

DALY, MARCUS (1937). *Big Game Hunting and Adventure 1897-1936.* Macmillan, London.

GRZIMEK, B. (1964). *Rhinos Belong to Everybody.* Collins, London.

GUGGISBERG, C A W. (1966) *SOS Rhino.* André Deutsch, London.

HUNTER, JOHN A. (1952). *Hunter.* Hamish Hamilton, London.

KRUUK, HANS (1972). *The Spotted Hyena – A Study of Predation and Social Behaviour.* University of Chicago Press, Chicago.

LOUTIT, BLYTHE (1988). The Damaraland Rhino, *African Wildlife*, vol. 42, no. 2, p. 66. Wildlife Society of Southern Africa, Cape Town.

MARTIN, ESMOND BRADLEY (1982). *Run Rhino Run.* Chatto & Windus, London.

MARTIN, ESMOND BRADLEY (1984). They're Killing Off The Rhino, *National Geographic*, vol. 165, no. 3, p. 404. National Geographic Society, Washington.

MARTIN, ESMOND BRADLEY (1988). Taiwan and the African rhino horn trade, *Swara*, vol 11, no. 6, p. 26; East African Wildlife Society, Nairobi.

OWEN-SMITH, NORMAN (1976). *The Behavioural Ecology of the White Rhino*, 3 vols. (Doctoral thesis)

OWEN-SMITH, NORMAN (1988). *Megaherbivores: The Influence of Very Large Body Size on Ecology.* Cambridge University Press, Cambridge.

PEASE, SIR ALFRED E. (reprint 1987). *The Book of the Lion.* St Martin's Press, New York.

PENNY, MALCOLM (1987). *Rhinos: Endangered Species.* Christopher Helm, London.

PLAYER, IAN (1972). *The White Rhino Saga.* Collins, London.

PRINGLE, JOHN (1982). *The Conservationists and The Killers.* Books of Africa (Pty) Ltd, Cape Town.

SELOUS, F C. (1893). *Travel & Adventure in South East Africa.* Rowland Ward & Co, London.

SELOUS, F C. (1908). *African Nature Notes and Reminiscences.* Macmillan, London.

SUTCLIFFE, ANTHONY J. (1985). *On the Track of Ice Age Mammals.* British Museum, London.

THOMPSON, RON (1986). *On Wildlife 'Conservation'.* United Publishers International, New York.

WAIT, ANETTE (1988). Ninety Percent of Africa's black rhino slaughtered, *Custos*, vol. 17, no. 8, p. 22. National Parks Board of South Africa, Pretoria.

A white rhino grazes on a hillside in Zululand's Umfolozi Game Reserve which today holds the world's largest concentration of these prehistoric-looking creatures. The Natal Parks Board's 'Operation Rhino' in the '60s centred around this reserve, and saved the white rhino from almost certain extinction. Earlier this century there were estimated to be as few as 30 white rhino left in southern Africa (all in the Umfolozi); today's world population of more than 4 600 of the southern subspecies (*Ceratotherium simum simum*) are probably all related to those hardy survivors.

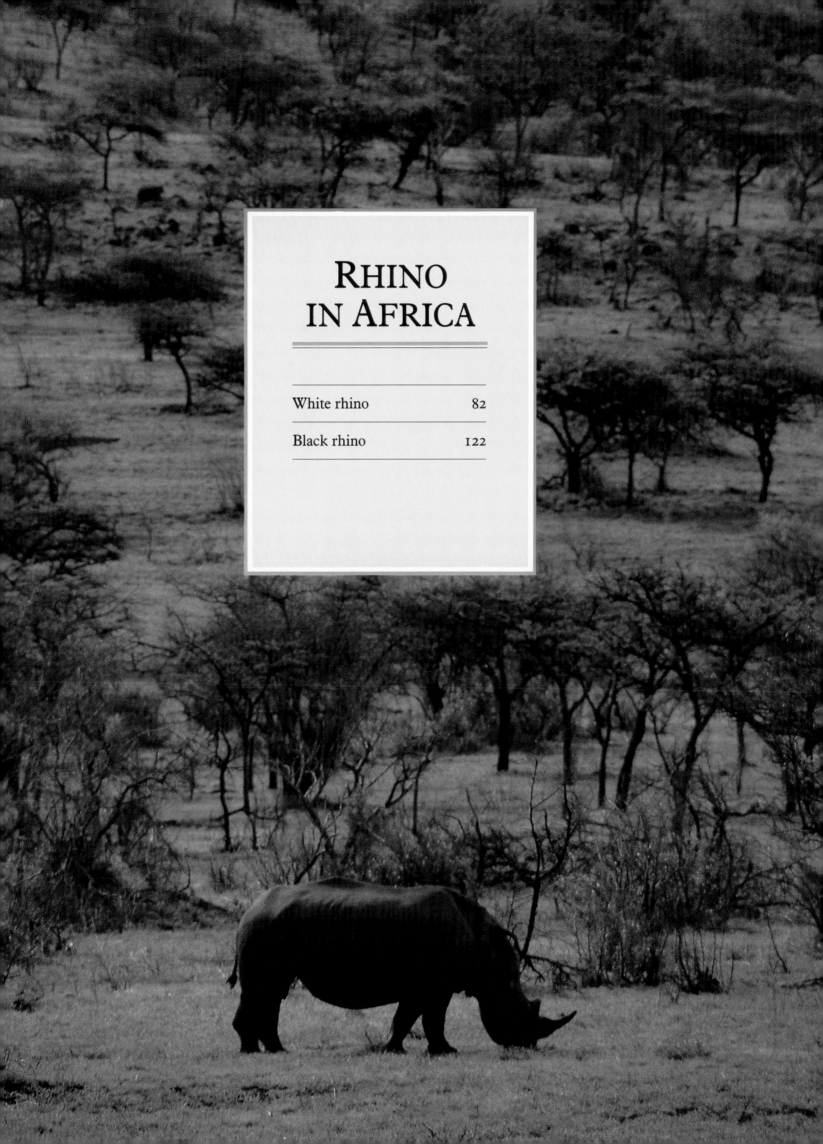

RHINO
IN AFRICA

The rhino's horn, evolved as a defensive weapon, is also its Achilles' heel and the reason for these animals having been hunted to the brink of extinction. Used for ornamental dagger handles in the Middle East and as an ingredient in traditional Oriental medicines for the treatment of pain and fever, the horn is in fact little more than compressed hair-like fibres (RIGHT) with a chemical composition similar to that of a fingernail. The demand for rhino horn – despite a worldwide ban on trade in rhino products – has led to a decline in world rhino numbers over the past 30 years from more than 100 000 to fewer than 12 000. Even the white rhino, previously considered relatively safe in the game reserves of South Africa (where the species is most abundant), is now being affected by illegal trade.

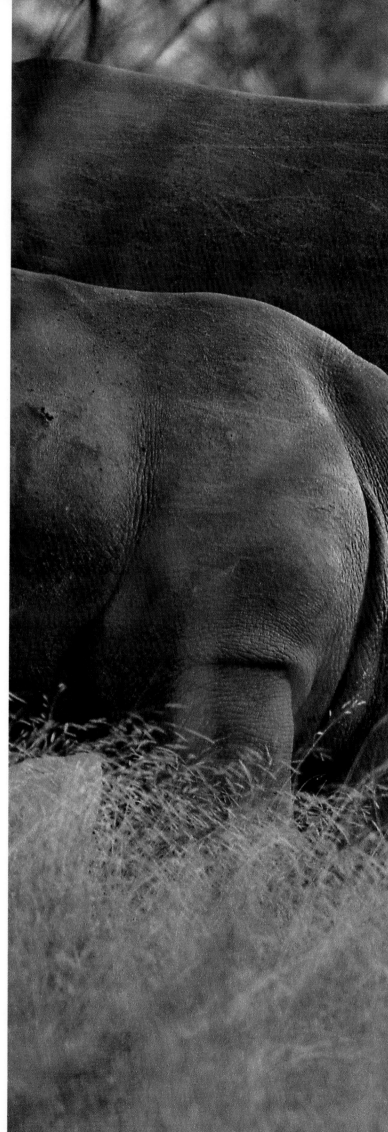

The largest of the five rhino species, white rhino are known for their timidity. Hampered by extreme short-sightedness but possessed of excellent hearing and a superb sense of smell, a close approach is possible if you take care to remain silently downwind. Although apparently engrossed in their feeding the rhino remain ever alert, their large trumpet-like ears flicking back and forth constantly; the slightest alien sound or whiff of human scent is likely to send them pounding off into the distance.

84

White rhino are exclusively grazers and have broad, square lips evolved specifically for cropping short grasses. This lip shape is a striking definitive feature and the source of one of the species' alternative common names, square-lipped rhino. White rhino prefer open grassland with short-grassed areas and trees and bush for shade and cover where they can spend the midday hours resting up.

OVERLEAF: The 'corridor' linking the Umfolozi and Hluhluwe game reserves is prime rhino country and it was a victory for conservation, and for rhino in particular, when the area was proclaimed a game reserve in 1989. This white rhino cow and her calf feed, oblivious to the political wrangling that went on over several decades before their homeland was made safe.

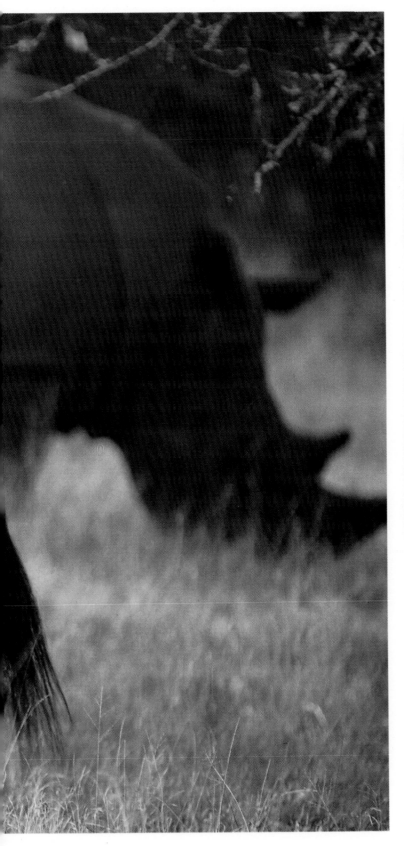

White rhino appear to tolerate the close proximity of most other animals even though they may compete for food with other grazing species. The blue wildebeest, impala and zebra are direct competitors, all enjoying the short grasses preferred by the white rhino, though the impala will also browse and thus supplement its diet.

While feeding competition among grazing species has little impact when times are good and early rains have brought a green flush to the brown and burnt grasses at the end of winter, in times of drought the white rhino can be seriously disadvantaged and game populations may have to be managed and manipulated.

Black and white rhino have little in common but appear to accept the presence of one another, though it's a rare occurrence to see the two species together like this. Fossil records indicate they evolved from a common ancestor, the white to become a grazer and the black predominantly a browser.

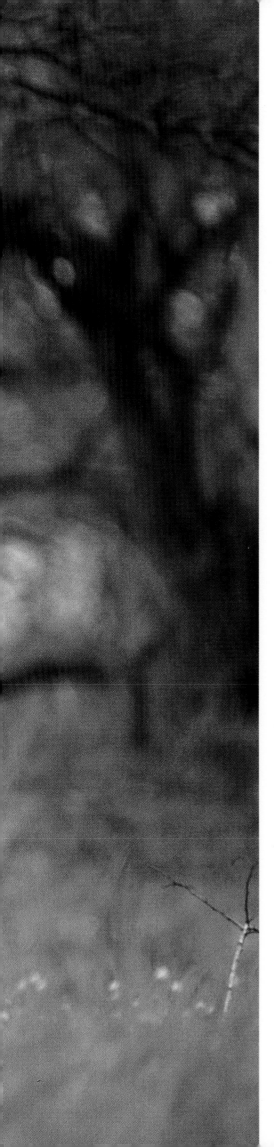

'Attaining a height of nearly seven feet at the shoulder, and carrying a cranium not dissimilar to a nine gallon cask; he flourishes upon the extremity of his square and truncated snout, a formidable weapon some three and a half feet long, fashioned after the approved method of a cobbler's awl, and capable, when wielded by a warrior so unquestionable in pith and renown, of being made to force its way through any opposition . . .' Sir William Cornwallis Harris in *Portraits of the Game and Wild Animals of Southern Africa* (1840).

The white rhino is the third-largest land mammal after the African and Indian elephants, but is no more white than the black rhino is black. All rhino tend to take on the colour of the mud of their last wallow, and the two African species cannot generally be distinguished by colour alone.

Rhino, unlike other grazing animals, are not gregarious, though the white rhino is frequently found in company with one or more other rhino (these groupings are usually temporary). Subadult animals (BELOW) frequently join up with each other and sometimes with an older 'auntie', probably for protection from predators.

White rhino adopt a distinctive defensive posture when they feel threatened or confused: members of the group stand in a circle with their tails together and their heads facing outward (LEFT).

Two white rhino bulls square up to each other in conflict over a cow in oestrus. While capable of inflicting serious harm and, frequently, death, most confrontations are settled with an elaborate display of ritualized bluffs and poses accompanied by a wide range of sounds and noises. After snorting and sparring with each other for more than an hour these combatants appeared to call a truce while all three animals took their midday nap (ABOVE).

All rhino bulls possess amazing sexual staying powers and may remain coupled with a cow for well over an hour at a time, with frequent and regular ejaculations – this aspect of these animals' behaviour is possibly the source of the myth that rhino horn is a powerful aphrodisiac. The cow takes the whole procedure in her stride, walking about and feeding, while the bull remains literally in tow, struggling to maintain his position and tottering along behind her on his hind legs. White rhino have a gestation period of 16 months, after which a single calf is born.

OVERLEAF: Rhino are generally more active at night than during the day, and begin moving towards their regular watering points at sundown.

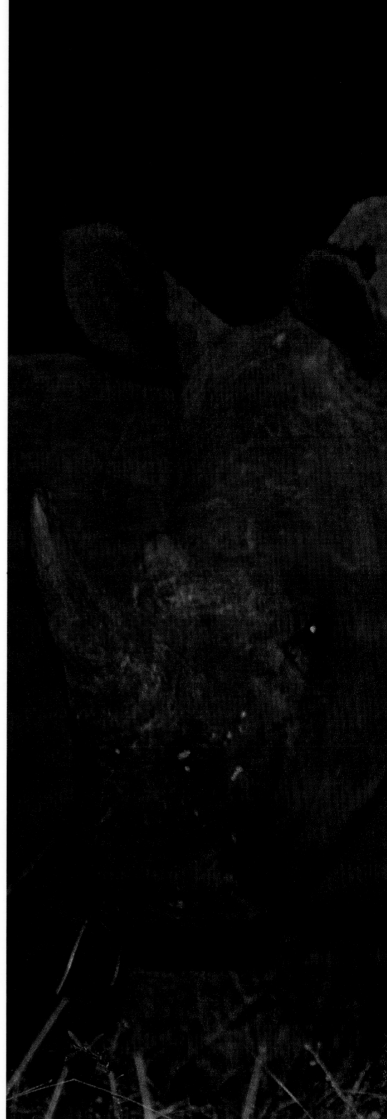

A lion yawns languorously as he prepares for the night's activities, while a herd of impala feed nervously nearby. White rhino are particularly active after dark, appearing to prefer the cool of night to the heat of the day. The peculiar grunts, snorts and squeals of the white rhino make an intriguing addition to the better-known sounds of the African night.

Water plays a vital role in the daily lives of Africa's largest mammals, for apart from quenching thirst it helps in keeping body temperatures down. Both rhino and elephant evidently derive great pleasure from their visits to the waterholes, which they seem to regard as social meeting places. Often, upon approaching a mud wallow, the rhino appear to test the consistency of the mud, shovelling it about with their snouts and stirring it up with their forefeet, before enjoying their ablutions (BELOW).

Hippo and crocodile abound in the waterways of Africa, but pose little threat to all but the smallest of rhino calves. Hippo and white rhino share the same feeding habits, preferring short, sweet grasses, which both animals can crop to a lawn-like evenness with their heavy, squared lower lips. Though rhino drink mainly at night, in the heat of summer they will make use of available water at all times of the day.

A young white rhino calf enjoys his midday snooze. Rhino spend a large part of their day
asleep or lolling about in mud wallows, which play a major role in both thermoregulation
and the control of pests such as ticks and flies. Even when asleep, the animals are fully alert,
ears twitching non-stop to discern any unnatural sounds.

Tails curled over their rumps, a rhino cow and her calf head away at a fast trot. A white rhino calf generally runs ahead of its mother, unlike the black rhino calf which follows behind. A warthog sow and her hoglets scurry about their business, appearing in many respects like miniature rhino.

Although white rhino calves begin grazing about a week after birth, they continue suckling from their mothers for as long as two years. Cute and inquisitive, white rhino young show intense curiosity about their surroundings. This brazen attitude is extended to other animals as well as rhino from outside the family group, and the calf will frequently challenge intruders (TOP LEFT) with the typical white rhino muzzle-to-muzzle stare.

Rhino are among the most magnificent and awe-inspiring creatures on earth. Massive, powerful, yet totally vulnerable to the whims of mankind, the survival of the world's few remaining rhino is one of the greatest challenges facing conservationists today.

In a world that is fast changing, mostly to the detriment of wildlife, the rhino have few allies. The diminutive oxpecker, a bird that feeds on the ticks and other parasites that infest the rhinos' hide, is perhaps their closest ally, giving early warning of the approach of man with a loud 'churr-churring' alarm call.

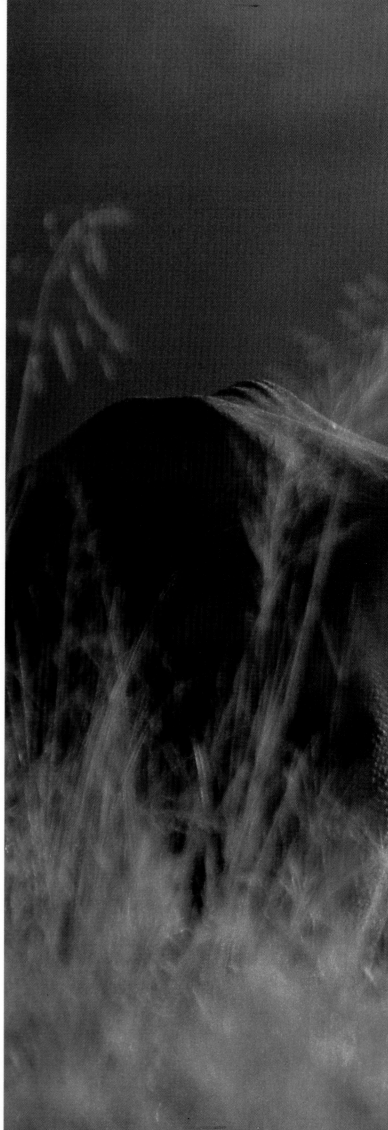

The vultures and hyaenas are the only winners in the war being waged against rhino by ruthless commercial poaching gangs. The incidence of poaching has escalated since the 1960s and Africa's rhino population has been decimated. Hunted for their horns and hide for centuries, fewer than 9 000 African rhino remain alive today compared with more than 100 000 only 30 years ago.

OVERLEAF: The white rhino is essentially a grazing animal, its broad, square-lipped mouth having evolved specifically for the purpose of cropping short grasses, as has its typical head-down stance. From a distance it is this stance that immediately distinguishes it from its smaller cousin the black rhino, along with its longer, narrower head and the pronounced nuchal hump on the back of its neck.

Although rhino are long gone from the north-western reaches of Botswana, rock art in the Tsodilo Hills shows that the early San 'Bushmen' of the region knew the animals, for they are well represented on the rock faces.

OVERLEAF: Black rhino have a reputation for naked aggression, belied by the frank curiosity displayed by this adult male and his young female companion. Unlike their white cousins, the black rhino will generally approach closely to investigate strange sounds or movements, the accompanying – and frightening – rush or 'charge' perhaps being responsible for their bad reputation.

Although solitary by nature, black rhino are often found in pairs comprising a mother and her calf, a relationship that extends until the birth of the next calf, usually for about five years. Temporary, larger aggregations as a result of feed and watering conditions may also be observed, but these are uncommon.

Formerly widely distributed throughout Africa, the black rhino was recorded as far south as the slopes of Table Mountain when the first white settlers arrived at the Cape in 1652. It is estimated that there could have been as many as a million black rhino on the plains of Africa last century: today fewer than 3 500 remain.

Like the luxuriantly coated nyala, black rhino are primarily browsers and feed on a wide variety of leaves, twigs and bark. Their prehensile upper lip functions like a dextrous finger, grasping and manipulating food into the mouth, and gives rise to one of their alternative common names, hook-lipped rhino.

Vincent, the one-eared rhino, was the first black rhino encountered by the authors and became a regular subject for their cameras. Black rhino appear to sustain damage to their ears more frequently than the other rhino species, perhaps because of their preference for dense, thorny habitats. Researchers in Kenya and Tanzania also postulate that black rhino calves lose their ears in tussles with hyaena, which grab the youngsters by their ears when attempting to prey on them. Black rhino calves, which run behind their mothers, suffer greater predation than white rhino young, which precede their mothers and are thus in a better position to be defended.

Black rhino are by nature curious creatures. Lucy's mum (TOP LEFT) was another regular subject and displayed a placid demeanour unusual in black rhino.

OVERLEAF: The hills and valleys of Zululand's game reserves are among the few safe refuges left for the rhino, but even here they are far from immune to the ravages of poaching.

Many black rhino in eastern and southern Africa have large, bleeding sores on their sides and chests. Caused by a *Stephanofilaria* parasite, these lesions appear to cause no discomfort, and disappear if the animal is translocated to an area where the parasite is not present. Ticks and flies are a rhino's constant companions. The black rhino was described as 'a swinish, cross-grained, ill-favoured, wallowing brute, with a hide like a rasp, an impudent cock of the chin, a roguish leer from out the corner of his eye, a mud-begrimed exterior and a necklace of ticks and horseflies,' by Cornwallis Harris in 1840.

Rhino make good use of suitable rocks, stumps and tree trunks, frequently polishing them to a glossy finish with their constant rubbing to rid themselves of ticks and other skin parasites. Yellowbilled oxpeckers live in a harmonious co-existence with large mammals such as rhino, giraffe and buffalo, feeding on the flies and ticks that infest their hides while serving as a superb early-warning system for their hosts.

Black rhino spend a large part of the day asleep, being most active in the cooler hours of early morning, late afternoon and night. Yawning like a sleepy child, a subadult (ABOVE) awakens from his afternoon nap.

In the summer rhino may spend hours basking in mud wallows which serve the function of regulating their body temperature as well as assisting in keeping tick infestations in control. The serrated hinged terrapin (*Pelusios sinuatos*), commonly found in waterholes, rivers and muddy wallows, takes the opportunity to nip ticks from the flanks of the resting rhino, and this species has even been observed on occasion biting at the raw lesions.

Like its white cousin, the black rhino is burdened with near-blindness but makes up for this with excellent senses of smell and hearing. Once its suspicions have been aroused, very little escapes its attention; when it has located the source of possible danger, it will in all probability charge headlong in that direction, pulling up at the last moment to inspect the effects of its actions. On numerous occasions, with the authors out of the way up a tree, the annoyed animal would stalk suspiciously right to the base of the tree, only to wheel away and retreat in panic once it had caught the human scent.

Rhino happily share their watering holes and wallows with other animals, such as these buffalo, and appear to be far more tolerant of each other here than anywhere else. Although wallowing has specific functions of temperature and pest regulation, rhino also appear to gain a simple hedonistic satisfaction from it, and their delight is quite obvious.

143

Although anti-social by nature, like most other animals such as these adolescent impala black rhino do have a ritualized greeting sequence that they employ when they cross paths, and meetings are rarely aggressive. These two adult cows (RIGHT) spent several minutes puffing and snorting before cautiously approaching each other to touch noses, while the youngsters, both males, sparred with each other for a while. After completing the social niceties all four settled down to rest in the shade of nearby trees, paying no further attention to one another. Usually encountered either singly or in pairs (a cow and her calf), groups such as this one (ABOVE) are occasionally formed, though they tend to arise out of feeding or drinking conditions rather than social needs.

145

Fire plays an important role in nature, burning off dead and dying undergrowth and clearing the way for new growth. Most fires tend to occur towards the end of the dry season and the first rains of spring soon ensure a healthy flush of tender new shoots. Black rhino appear unfazed by the blackened landscape, and relish the charred remains of acacia scrub. Regular burning as a management policy keeps parts of the Umfolozi-Hluhluwe-Corridor complex ideally vegetated for black rhino habitation. While fire can kill smaller and slower creatures, such as this leopard tortoise investigating an *Ammocharis* flower, baboons delight in scouring the burnt larder.

OVERLEAF: Black rhino appear able to adapt to life in harsh environments and seem capable of withstanding drought or desert conditions better than most as long as suitable browse is available.

146

Although not territorial to the extent of the white rhino, black rhino bulls do utilize urine-spraying to advertise their presence in an area. Black rhino show little difference in size or horn conformation between sexes, and it is impossible to sex them accurately without a clear rear view (TOP LEFT).

The reasons for the black rhino's dung scattering, which it does by vigorously kicking backwards with its hind legs, are not fully understood, although there are numerous legends which explain the activity. Although they utilize communal dung heaps, or middens – often the same one used by white rhino – this behaviour does not appear to have any territorial significance, perhaps acting merely as a social indicator. Dung beetles, which lay their eggs in the ball of excreta before burying it, defend the fruits of their labour vigorously from a piratical rival intent on hijacking dungball and female in one fell swoop (ABOVE).

Black rhino cows and their calves display strong bonds, and mothers will defend their offspring ferociously. Adult bulls show marked aggression towards young animals, and cause a high mortality rate among infants in areas of high black rhino densities.

Having discerned the authors' presence, the cow and her calf stalked cautiously closer. Both animals appeared fascinated by the figures in the tree – where the authors had by then sought safety from the advancing pair – and stood right below them, gingerly sniffing at the tree trunk, where the scent of their arch-enemies, man, must surely have lingered . . . Encounters such as this were of special significance to the authors, and brought them spiritually closer to their subjects.

Black rhino suffer little predation from anyone but man, though lion have been known to pull down adults on rare occasions. While smaller cats such as leopard and cheetah stand little chance of killing even small calves, hyaena regularly do so. Black rhino show little tolerance towards the larger predators, and lions appear to show a certain respect for the crusty warriors and keep well clear of the lethal horn.

OVERLEAF: While most rhino will drink on a daily basis, the desert black rhino (*D.b. bicornis*) found in inhospitable terrain in Namibia can survive without water for three or four days.

Kenya's black rhino population has fallen from 20 000 to about 200 over the past 30 years, due primarily to poachers hunting the species to satisfy the demand for rhino horn. Kenya and Tanzania appear to have borne the brunt of the poaching pressure since the 1960s, both countries having lost more than 95 per cent of their rhino. This tragic loss can be ascribed both to the unusually large horns carried by the species in the region and ineffective patrolling and policing of the game reserves as a result of a lack of money and manpower. Today most surviving black rhino in Kenya are in well-guarded fenced sanctuaries, many having been relocated from more vulnerable areas, or on private game farms.

OVERLEAF: The classic East African view of black rhino in Amboseli National Park in Kenya, the snow-capped peak of Mount Kilimanjaro creating a magnificent backdrop, is today becoming a thing of the past as unprecedented poaching decimates East Africa's rhino populations.

RHINO IN ASIA

The Indian rhino with its primitive, armoured and studded appearance differs from its
African cousins in having only one horn. Seriously endangered, some 2 000 of the species
survive in several parks and reserves in India and Nepal, where they appear to be receiving
effective protection. Water-loving animals, Indian rhino are good swimmers and are never
found far from water, their preferred habitat being dense thickets surrounding swampy areas.
PREVIOUS SPREAD: An Indian rhino in a *jheel*, a muddy seasonal waterhole, in the Royal
Chitawan National Park, Nepal.

Anti-social in the extreme, Indian rhino are known for their aggression. Fights between members of the species are common, the animals biting with their long, sharp incisors rather than using their short, blunt horns. Indian rhino are grazers as well as browsers, with as much as 80 per cent of their diet being grass, the balance comprising cane shoots, shrubs, leaves, fruits and agricultural crops where available.

The Indian rhino is not territorial and does not use the urine-spraying technique of scent-marking common in the white and black rhino, although it does make use of middens. These appear not to have any territorial significance and are probably used merely to advise other rhino of a rhino's presence in the area.

The Sumatran rhino is the smallest of all the rhino species, and probably also the least evolved. It is covered with dense, dark hair that has given it the name of 'buffalo rhino' among local hunters and is not all that different in appearance from the forest rhino which disappeared during the Ice Age some 15000 years ago. Secretive and unsociable, the species has not been studied successfully in the wild, and only two living specimens exist in zoos outside of its homeland.

174

A Javan rhinoceros photographed in the Ujung Kulon
National Park, Java, in 1963.

Index